ADVANCE PRAISE FOR **THE GOURMET DAD**

"What I love about Dean's family fare is that it is not dumbed down for kids. These meals and sides and vegetables are fun, interactive, flavorful and creative. The secret to conquering picky eaters is to build their palates from an early age and get them involved in the meal. Dean is clever with dippers for veggies and healthy twists on classic comfort foods that make the dishes more nutritious while introducing kids to a wide range of adult flavors. The only problem with Dean's recipes will be choosing which one your family wants to eat first."

—**RACHAEL RAY**

"Dean McDermott is indeed the Gourmet Dad! He really makes me want to cook and I can barely open a can of soup for my kids. I'm forever taking them out to eat and I can see their long faces saying 'not again, Dad!' But with Dean's incredible recipes and salivating dishes I'm tempted to stay in and cast myself as 'The Gourmet Dad.'"

—**DYLAN MCDERMOTT**

"I love Dean's approach to cooking for his family. Keep it simple, keep it fun, keep it tasty. He's bringing back the Sunday dinner."

—**CHEF MARK MCEWAN**

"This book really captures the sense of humor, generosity and dedication to food and family that drives Dean every single day. It's playful and inspiring—and everyone could always use a little more of that to brighten their days."

—**ROGER MOOKING**

"One of the very best things you can do for your family is cook for them and with Dean McDermott's beautiful new cookbook you'll discover how simple it is to impress yourself in your own kitchen!"

—**CHEF MICHAEL SMITH**

"You definitely don't need kids to love the recipes in this book! Dean has mastered the art of cooking AND presentation which makes this a MUST HAVE for entertaining!"

—**MARIA MENOUNOS**

The GOURMET DAD

EASY *and* DELICIOUS MEALS THE WHOLE FAMILY WILL *Love*

DEAN McDERMOTT

Foreword by **GUY FIERI**   Photography by **JAMES TSE**

THE GOURMET DAD
ISBN-13: 978-0-373-89289-1
© 2015 by Dean McDermott

Library of Congress Cataloging-in-Publication Data
McDermott, Dean, 1966-
  The gourmet dad : easy and delicious recipes the whole family will love / Dean McDermott ; foreword by Guy Fieri ; photography by James Tse.
     pages cm
  Includes index.
  ISBN 978-0-373-89289-1 (alk. paper)
   Cooking. I. Title.
  TX714.M3823 2014
  641.5--dc 3
                              2013050673

www.Harlequin.com

Printed in U.S.A.

Design: Alissa Faden
Photography: James Tse

This book is for the two most important women in my life.

My Mom, Doreen. She set me on this cooking path, and I am forever grateful. And my beautiful wife, Tori. Thank you for your undying love, support and inspiration, and also for the beautiful family you gave me, which I get to cook for. I'm truly blessed. I love you.

CONTENTS

Chapter seven
A LITTLE ON THE SIDE 157

Chapter eight
THE SWEET STUFF 177

Foreword

ALL THAT I EVER REALLY WANTED TO DO WAS (1) BE A GREAT DAD AND (2) COOK FOR A LIVING. BUT DON'T GET ME WRONG, I'VE ALWAYS KNOWN THAT BOTH OF THESE THINGS ARE TOUGH TO ACCOMPLISH.

That I've been balancing the chef—dad duties for a while now is an understatement. But let me tell you, I don't regret one minute of the long hours, hard work or late nights to do my best at raising two great boys and keeping my kitchens going.

So, when Food Network talked to me about partnering up with my sister-from-another-mister, Rachael Ray, for *Rachael vs. Guy: Celebrity Cook Off,* I was a little bit skeptical. I mean, I'm a chef...I landed on TV by *accident.* Why on earth would a real celebrity want to embarrass him or herself cooking on TV? So, did I think a random (but hugely successful) bunch of actors, musicians and athletes could get in the kitchen and cook it up in a way that would make Rachael and me proud? Probably not. But I was in for a surprise.

On day one of RvG, Season 2, I met Dean McDermott and thought all right, nice enough guy, looks like some kind of movie star and from what I hear, he's got a big-time reality show. Uh, yeah, I'm sure he can cook...riiiight.

Well, when I tell you that Dean blew me away, it would be downplaying it. Not only did this dude have some serious culinary skills, he had a competitive fire that I immediately saw as a huge advantage in the competition. Then, we got to talking about what really makes him tick and he told me about his whole Gourmet Dad angle. We talked all about his kids, Jack, Liam, Stella, Hattie and little Finn (with whom Tori was on bed rest during the production). We talked about how our lives changed when we had our kids and how cooking and food really, to both of us, are of the utmost importance in our philosophy of how to raise our kids. I didn't see Dean as this big, tattooed, movie star kind of cat anymore. He was a dad. A great dad. Who, like me, is passionately devoted to cooking for and with his kids to teach them about nutrition, how to have a healthy relationship with food and sometimes, above all, to make them smile.

Dean went on to win the second season for Team Guy and launch into a culinary career of his own. His creativity and passionate pursuit of being the Gourmet Dad have not only inspired me but millions of people, through his website and TV special *Dean & Tori's Backyard Bash* that I executive produced for Cooking Channel. And now, with this book, *The Gourmet Dad,* you can take Dean's passion home, into your own kitchen, and let him help your family really get cookin'. His recipes are easy and fun but still really rockin'. And best of all, the whole family will want to get involved. And that's the beauty of *The Gourmet Dad.*

Love, Peace & Taco Grease,

Guy

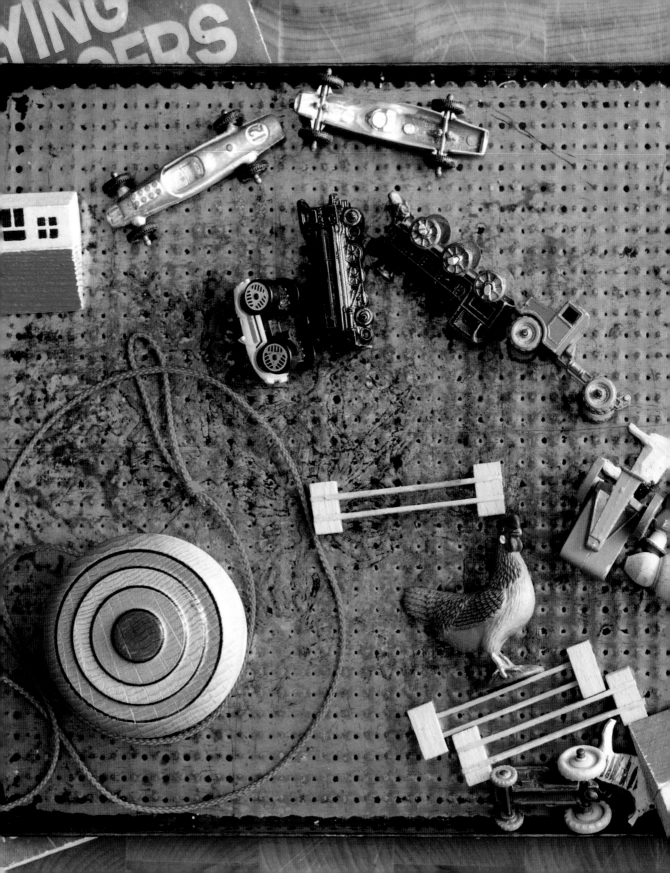

Introduction

MOST PEOPLE KNOW ME AS AN ACTOR/TV PERSONALITY FROM MY ROLES

on *Due South, Without a Trace, Open Range* or *NCIS,* or they recognize me from my hit reality TV show, *Tori & Dean: Home Sweet Hollywood*. But my favorite—and most important—role is Dad to five of the best munchkins in the world: Jack, Liam, Stella, Hattie and Finn. Along with my wife, Tori, they make up my world and my cooking audience. I've made it my mission to use my cooking expertise to come up with meals the kids (and Tori and I) love. I want them to grow up understanding how important nutrition is, but also appreciating what a blast cooking and eating really great food can be. When it comes to kids and getting them on board, it's as much about the presentation and the use of little tricks to make food interactive as it is about the food itself.

My experiences cooking for the McDermott clan led to my starting The Gourmet Dad website and, ultimately, to writing this book. But the experiences that led me to love food actually happened decades ago.

I grew up in Toronto, Canada, with three sisters, a wonderful mom who wasn't quite Julia Child, and a dad who wasn't quite Ward Cleaver. We were at the lower end of the economic scale—we weren't *The Trailer Park Boys,* but we scraped by on a fixed income and lived in government-subsidized housing. That meant some very creative cooking on any given night to stretch what was in the cupboards to make dinner for six. But it also meant that my mom was dead set on training me to be a gentleman who was ready for a higher station in life. She insisted that a true man knows how to take care of himself, how to clean and how to cook. I was always my mom's sous-chef. I peeled potatoes, kneaded dough, and got to lick the chocolate off the wooden spoon we used to make boxed chocolate cake. (Unfortunately, that spoon was the same one used to paddle my behind when I was bad—which was more often than I care to admit. I had a real love/hate relationship with that spoon. . . .)

I got so comfortable in the kitchen that one day I decided to fly solo. I can still see it clearly, my nine-year-old self strutting into the middle of the living room and announcing, "I'm going to make dinner!" Nobody was more surprised than me. What was I thinking? Did my brain just hear what my mouth was saying? And what was I going to make?

All I knew was that I wanted it to be good, and I wanted it to be all my creation. My menu included a hollowed-out Italian roll filled with ground beef, mozzarella, Parmesan and a tomato-basil sauce and a side of garlic pasta. There was a whole idea behind the dish. I figured people could mix the beef mixture with their pasta or use the chunks of bread left over from the rolls for dipping. It was presentation meets function with a side of deliciousness.

I served up six plates and waited, holding my breath. And guess what? Instant hit. Everybody loved it, and every last morsel was polished off by the end of dinner. I was incredibly satisfied. It meant so much to me that I had created something good and it had made my family happy. I wanted to re-create that feeling again and again. I think that's how a lot of chefs get started.

I was hooked. I started experimenting with my mom, trying out different dishes, including new desserts. After my mom passed away, I meandered through life, trying to find my way. I was living with my sister Dawn and her family, and I desperately needed a part-time job. After several

failed attempts to get the jobs I wanted, I accepted a dishwashing position at a big chain steak house that was just opening its doors. It was hard, wet, messy work, but I loved it. I'd go to work after school, where I was studying drama, and go home at 2:00 a.m. the next morning, soaking wet, with feet like prunes.

Once I graduated from high school, I started working full-time at the restaurant. I'd prep during the day and cook on the line at night. I eventually became the first cook and would pick up odd shifts as a waiter, bartender or host. I did it all. It was an incredible experience, and I've used those skills more times than I could ever possibly count.

But no cooking experience has made me as happy as cooking for my family. When I first started dating Tori, we'd go out to really nice restaurants and eat wonderful meals. We quickly found our favorite places to go and our favorite dishes on the menu. Madly in love, we would ogle each other as well as our food. True foodies in true love.

That all changed when we started having kids. It wasn't so easy to find the time, opportunity or energy to go out, but we still wanted to enjoy those meals and I'd be darned if I were going to give them up. So I started making our favorite meals at home. As the kids got older (and more plentiful), I started working on ways to adapt these meals into ones the kids would eat. I was dead set on making sure my kids didn't become finicky eaters. You can't win them all, but you've got to try. I wanted them to enjoy food and treasure the experience of family meals, like I had. I've always wanted to give my kids the gift of Sunday dinner memories and the kind of rich food-related traditions that they could hand down to their kids.

The more I created new dishes, and variations for kids, the more other parents asked me for advice and recipes. I found out that all parents face similar challenges. Schedules are tight. Kids need to get dressed and get to school; there are errands that have be tackled, soccer games that need to be coordinated, playdates, grocery shopping; and, oh yeah, the upstairs toilet isn't working, again. And unless they're part of the lucky minority, most parents are going to deal with the dreaded finicky eater or the specific preferences of different children and at different ages. One kid will eat only mac and cheese, while the other is apparently on a diet of applesauce and chicken nuggets. In my house, and if I had to make one more batch of butter noodles, my head was going to explode.

I started The Gourmet Dad to teach parents, and even single adults, that putting a gourmet dinner on the table doesn't require a chef's hat or training, or seven free hours in your day. We can all eat like restaurant diners, even when we don't have the time, money, inclination or energy to head out to our favorite eatery. I also wanted to show people that it's possible to have fun in the kitchen with your kids and to help them develop their palates beyond the world of chicken nuggets.

I want to tear down the wall that differentiates adult food from kids' food. Growing up, we kids all ate the same thing as Mom and Dad and we ate as a family. One table, no TV. Just food, family and fun.

In the pages that follow, you'll find recipes meant to save you time, stress and the hassle of being a short-order cook, while still putting delicious and memorable meals on the table. Most include a kid version, or simple tweaks and strategies for adapting the dish to a child's palate. I've added a few recipes here and there that are just for adults. And I've included the occasional recipe that is a little more on the adventurous side. These I've labeled "Stella's Choice," because Stella is the most adventurous eater among my five. Throughout the book, I've sprinkled in some tips and stories that I hope will help make your time in the kitchen easier, more enjoyable, more successful and, most of all, *fun!*

Chapter one

GREEN STUFF

Growing up poor, we never bought fresh fruits and vegetables—just canned or frozen. As a result, our veggies were always mushy, overcooked and tasteless. My mom never knew the terms *blanch* and *sauté*. Bless her heart, she would open a can, dump it in a pan, and boil the crap out of it. And it didn't help that my dad was a strict meat-and-potatoes Scotsman who thought vegetables were "rabbit food."

It wasn't until I was in my late twenties that I discovered how great fresh vegetables were and how many ways there were to prepare them. And it wasn't until I went to culinary school, at the ripe old age of forty-three, that I really learned to love veggies and how to cook them properly. It was a real eye-opener.

I was determined that when I had kids of my own, they wouldn't have to wait until they were adults to appreciate fresh vegetables. Health benefits aside, the right vegetables cooked in the right way are just plain delicious, and I want my kids to experience them that way, too. Easier said than done. To make sure everyone in the house eats as many veggies as possible, I've developed what a friend calls "Deano's Bag of Tricks."

They're not really tricks so much as strategies. (I don't like the idea of "tricking" kids. With the right encouragement they should honestly come to appreciate vegetables—and all kinds of different foods—for their own unique flavors.) These strategies can be as simple as cutting up the green beans you're making for your own dinner into bite-size pieces and using them as "rocks" for an ocean reef salad seascape on your child's plate. I use broccoli or asparagus as trees, and carrots as chicken beaks, and I carve faces out of sweet potatoes. Point is, eating in my house is as fun as it is nutritious. And, most importantly, it's interactive. Why shouldn't it be?

In this chapter I'll teach you how to make vegetable dishes both you and your kids will love. I've included ways to make each of these dishes fun and interesting for the little ones, while still cooking killer meals for the adults in the house. Let's get our green on and get creative.

ASPARAGUS AND PANCETTA SALAD

This is a pretty simple but super-satisfying salad. The secret is the pancetta, the ultimate bacon, Italian-style. Not only is it a key addition to this salad, but I also use the rendered fat from cooking the pancetta to make a savory, rich vinaigrette. If you're not into rendered fat, you can always use olive oil. How you cook the pancetta is critical: it should be golden and crispy on the outside, but the interior should still be moist. Proper preparation is also essential for the asparagus spears, which are blanched—a process of quick cooking that locks in nutrients and preserves the fresh flavor and vibrant color of vegetables. This is a one-of-a-kind salad and a perfect brunch entrée.

SERVES 4

1. Fill a large pot three-quarters full of water and bring it to a rolling boil over medium-high heat. Add the salt.

2. Fill a large bowl with enough water to cover the asparagus spears once they are cooked, and add enough ice to chill the water completely.

3. Drop the asparagus spears into the boiling water, reduce the heat to medium and cook until they turn bright green, 2 to 5 minutes. Transfer the asparagus to the ice bath to stop the cooking process and maintain the green color.

4. Heat a heavy cast-iron skillet over medium heat. Place the pancetta in the skillet, reduce the heat to medium-low and render the pancetta fat (allow it to become liquid). When the pancetta is crisp, remove it to a paper towel–lined plate to drain and set aside. Reserve the rendered fat in the skillet.

5. Add the shallots to the rendered fat in the skillet and sauté over medium heat until just soft, about 3 minutes.

6. In a small bowl, whisk together the mustard and vinegar until smooth. Slowly add the shallots and the fat from the skillet, whisking until incorporated. Depending on how much fat was rendered, you may need to adjust your vinaigrette by adding oil.

7. Arrange the pea tendrils in a medium bowl, pour the warm vinaigrette over them and toss gently to coat (the tendrils should wilt slightly). Season with salt and pepper.

3 tablespoons salt

20 asparagus spears

5 slices slab (unrolled) pancetta, diced (or substitute smoked bacon)

1 small shallot, peeled and minced

1 heaping tablespoon beer mustard (or substitute a grainy Dijon mustard)

1 tablespoon apple cider vinegar

2 cups fresh pea tendrils (or substitute pea shoots)

Kosher salt and freshly cracked black pepper, to taste

¼ cup shaved aged pecorino cheese

¼ cup toasted sourdough bread crumbs, tossed with 1 tablespoon olive oil

8. Place half the asparagus on a serving platter. Cover with a layer of pea tendrils, pecorino and bread crumbs. Top with the crisped pancetta. Repeat with the remaining ingredients, and serve and enjoy!

FOR THE kiddos

You can keep all the vegetable goodness of this salad and still make it a kid-pleasing favorite by repurposing the ingredients, dialing back on some of the more unusual elements and flavors, and presenting the dish in a way that's more familiar to the little ones. The secret? Dipping sauce!

1 In a medium bowl, combine all the ingredients for the dipping sauce and stir until well mixed. Set aside. Preheat the broiler on high.

2 Melt the butter in a medium skillet over medium heat. Sauté the blanched asparagus and snap peas until hot, 4 to 5 minutes. Add the pancetta and ¼ cup of the Parmesan and toss to coat. Transfer to a baking sheet, leaving enough room to accommodate the bread.

3 Adjust the top rack of the oven so that it is about 6 inches away from the broiler flame. Brush the bread with the olive oil. Sprinkle 1 tablespoon of grated cheese on each slice. Arrange the slices alongside the asparagus mixture on the baking sheet.

4 Place the baking sheet under the broiler, and broil until the cheese on the bread has melted and the bread is toasted, about 3 to 4 minutes. Watch it carefully. Remove and let cool for 2 minutes.

5 Cut the bread slices into thirds, and spoon the asparagus mixture on top. Serve with the dipping sauce on the side.

Dipping Sauce
- ¼ cup mayonnaise
- ¼ cup Greek yogurt
- 2 tablespoons grated Parmesan cheese
- 1 teaspoon yellow mustard

Salad
- 2 tablespoons unsalted butter
- 10 asparagus spears, blanched and cut into 1-inch pieces
- 1 cup snap peas, trimmed and blanched
- 3 slices slab (unrolled) pancetta, finely diced and rendered extra crispy
- ¼ cup grated Parmesan cheese, plus 2 tablespoons for garnish
- 2 slices sourdough bread
- 2 teaspoons olive oil

ARUGULA SALAD WITH "QUICKLED" GINGER
and Crispy Shallots

Life is too short to be boring or bland. That's why I use pickled ginger in this salad (and just about anywhere else I can fit it in). Pickled ginger can be used as a vibrant condiment on sandwiches, burgers and fish tacos, as an ingredient in salads and salad dressings, and as an accompaniment to sushi. I have a rainbow of colors, flavors and textures in this salad, but I especially love the arugula, because it adds just a hint of peppery freshness. You can create a truly beautiful presentation and do the salad proud by serving it in radicchio cups.

SERVES 4 TO 6

1. Combine all the "quickled" ingredients except the ginger in a large pot with 5 cups of water and bring to a boil over medium-high heat. Remove from the heat and let the liquid cool slightly. Place the ginger in a large bowl and pour the liquid over it. Let cool to room temperature and then refrigerate. It will keep for up to 2 weeks in the refrigerator.

2. In a small bowl, combine the shallots, orange juice and sesame oil and marinate for 5 minutes. Add the rest of the vinaigrette ingredients to the shallot–orange juice mixture and whisk until completely combined. Set aside.

continued on next page >>>

Dean's Food 411

The best way to include citrus in a salad is to cut it into "supremes." These are trimmed pieces of the fruit's flesh, with no white rind (pith) or other remnants of the peel. To supreme a piece of citrus, slice off the ends so that the flesh is visible on the top and bottom. Set the fruit on one end and use a sharp knife to carve off the peel and rind, following the curve of the fruit. Try to remove just the pith and leave as much flesh as possible. Once you're done, you'll see the vertical white membranes that separate each segment. Cut alongside the membranes on each side of a segment to slice out a wedge of fruit. Repeat until all the segments have been freed from the membranes. Do it right and you'll wind up with beautiful uniform pieces of fruit that are juicy and flavorful. For a video showing this procedure, go to www.thegourmetdad.com.

"Quickled" (Quick Pickled) Ginger

- ½ cup rice wine vinegar
- 5 tablespoons kosher salt
- 1 teaspoon whole coriander seeds
- 1 teaspoon crushed red pepper flakes
- 1 teaspoon black peppercorns
- 1 teaspoon whole cloves
- ½ teaspoon allspice berries
- 1 bay leaf
- 1 cup peeled and thinly sliced (paper-thin) fresh ginger

Vinaigrette

- ½ shallot, peeled and minced
  Juice of 1 orange
- ½ tablespoon sesame oil
- 1 tablespoon soy sauce
- 1 tablespoon minced fresh tarragon
  Salt and freshly cracked black pepper, to taste

Salad

- ½ cup olive oil
- 5 shallots, peeled and sliced into thin rings
  Salt and freshly cracked black pepper, to taste
  Pinch of cayenne pepper
- 4 cups arugula
- 2 oranges, supremed (see box)
- 1 bunch frisée (or substitute radicchio or a bitter green)
- 1 scallion, root end removed and cut diagonally into thin slices
- 2 tablespoons sesame seeds, lightly toasted

3. In a heavy pan or a cast-iron skillet, heat the olive oil over medium-high heat. Add the shallots and fry until crispy, about 5 minutes. Remove with a slotted spoon or skimmer to a paper towel–lined small bowl. Season at once with salt, black pepper and cayenne pepper and set aside.

4. Combine the arugula, oranges, frisée, scallions and sesame seeds in a large salad bowl and toss gently. Add the reserved shallots, the "quickled" ginger and the reserved vinaigrette and toss the salad until it is well coated.

FOR THE kiddos

To make this more appetizing for the young tongue and imagination, I serve it as a rock 'n' roll jellyfish. It's pretty much the same salad, just simplified and with milder flavors. Add rice or pasta to make this a more filling dish or a complete meal.

SERVES 2

1 Combine the vinaigrette ingredients in a small bowl and whisk to blend thoroughly.

2 Toss together the romaine, the crispy shallots and the "quickled" ginger in a large bowl. Coat sparingly with the vinaigrette and season with a little salt. Next, spread the salad on a serving plate. This will be the ocean floor.

3 Spread out the arugula leaves evenly on the plate to mimic seaweed. Arrange the orange supremes (the "fishes") on the plate, and sprinkle the sesame seeds over the finished seascape.

Vinaigrette

Juice of 1 orange

¼ cup sesame oil

1 teaspoon honey

1 teaspoon soy sauce

Salad

½ head romaine lettuce, thinly sliced

1 tablespoon crispy shallots (from step 3 of adult recipe)

1 tablespoon "quickled" ginger, slivered

Salt, to taste

8 arugula leaves

1 orange, supremed (see box on page 6)

1 tablespoon sesame seeds, lightly toasted

GREEN BEAN AND PURPLE CABBAGE SLAW
with Garlicky Tomato Vinaigrette

I find that a lot of people just don't know what to do with purple cabbage, so they end up not using it at all. It was a staple in my dad's house when he was growing up in Cabbagetown in Toronto, Canada. Cabbage was a very popular, healthy and cheap food among the immigrants that populated the area. With thirteen kids to feed, my grandma knew how to stretch a cabbage at mealtime. Purple cabbage is a terrific addition to salads and dishes of all kinds, and kids love the color and crunchy texture. Plus, purple cabbage is sturdy enough to cut into fun shapes with a knife or cookie cutter. If you chop it or shred it up well, even your youngest will chow down on it (and will eat the green beans in this slaw in the process). If you or anybody else in the family just doesn't like purple cabbage, substitute savoy cabbage, radicchio or endive.

SERVES 4

1. Preheat the oven to 400°F.

2. Cut the tomatoes in half and toss them with the garlic, salt and pepper in a small bowl. Drizzle with the 2 tablespoons olive oil, or just enough to coat them, spread them out on a baking sheet and sprinkle with the thyme.

3. Roast the tomatoes and garlic until the tomatoes start to blister and open up, about 7 minutes. Remove from the oven, drizzle with the vinegar and let cool. Once cool, remove the garlic and lightly mash it.

4. Scrape all contents into a medium bowl and gently whisk in the remaining ½ cup of olive oil, keeping the vinaigrette nice and chunky. Season with salt, pepper, ancho chili powder and sugar.

5. In a large salad bowl, combine the green beans, cabbage, scallions, the 3 ounces feta, the ⅛ cup almonds and the ½ tablespoon parsley and toss gently. Drizzle with the vinaigrette and toss again. Taste and season with salt and pepper.

6. Arrange the salad on individual salad plates. Garnish each with the remaining ounce of feta, ⅛ cup almonds and ½ tablespoon parsley. Serve at once.

Vinaigrette

2 cups cherry tomatoes

6 cloves garlic

Salt and pepper, to taste

2 tablespoons olive oil, plus ½ cup

Leaves from 6 sprigs fresh thyme

2 tablespoons red wine vinegar

2 teaspoons ancho chili powder, or to taste

Pinch of granulated sugar

Slaw

⅔ pound green beans, ends trimmed, halved diagonally, and blanched (page 173)

½ head purple cabbage, cored and shredded or thinly sliced

3 scallions, root ends removed and cut diagonally into thin slices

3 ounces crumbled feta cheese, plus 1 ounce for garnish

⅛ cup sliced almonds, plus ⅛ cup for garnish

½ tablespoon minced fresh parsley, plus ½ tablespoon for garnish

Salt and pepper, to taste

FOR THE kiddos

Want your children to gobble up this slaw? Give them the green light to make face
at the table—or at least to eat one. The key to the kids' version of this dish is dialing back o
some of the stronger flavors, like onions, garlic and chili powder.

SERVES 4

1   Reduce the amount of garlic to 1 clove and the chili powder to just a pinch for the vinaigrette and blend until smooth in a blender or food processor.

2   For the slaw, keep the ingredients separate, add fresh cherry tomatoes, and replace half
of the cabbage with shredded or chopped romaine lettuce. Leave out the scallions and
parsley. Do not dress the slaw.

3   Create a person on each salad plate. Mix the cabbage and romaine together for the hair.
Slice two cherry tomatoes in half and add almonds to create eyes. Make a mouth and
hands out of the remaining almonds, and use green beans for the body and arms. Use the
feta as a neck or shirt. (You can also create a cool jellyfish with the ingredients, using the
green beans for the tentacles, for example.) Kids can pull apart bits and pieces and dip
them into the vinaigrette. It's a surefire way to get them to eat their veggies!

SEARED SCALLOPS, SHAVED APPLES AND FENNEL
with Roasted Shallot Vinaigrette

Want a fancy restaurant-quality meal at home? Something perfect for date night (I think I remember what that is....)? Well, here it is. Seared scallops always make for a sophisticated presentation, and the searing process draws out and emphasizes the naturally sweet flavors of this shellfish. There is a lot to keep a tongue happy with this dish, and a sparkling vinaigrette is the icing on the cake.

SERVES 4

1. Preheat the oven to 400°F.

2. Spread the shallots on a baking sheet. Drizzle with 2 tablespoons of the olive oil, and season with salt and pepper. Sprinkle with the thyme and 2 sprigs' worth of the rosemary. Roast the shallots until tender, 10 to 12 minutes.

3. Allow the roasted shallots to cool before mincing them. Combine them with the remaining rosemary, orange juice, lemon juice and zest, and garlic in a small bowl and mix well. Whisk in the remaining ½ cup olive oil and season the vinaigrette with salt and pepper.

4. Pat the scallops dry and allow them to come to room temperature. In the meantime, combine the apple, fennel, lemon juice and lemon halves in a medium bowl and set aside.

5. Preheat a large sauté pan over high heat. Using a sharp knife, score the top of each scallop in a crisscross pattern and season both sides with salt, pepper and a drizzle of grapeseed oil.

6. When the pan is hot, carefully place the scallops in it with the crisscross side down. Do not move the scallops until they release from the pan, about 3 to 4 minutes. This will give you the best sear and coloring.

7. Once the crisscross side releases and is golden brown, flip the scallops and add the butter. Once the butter has melted, baste the scallops a few times and then remove the pan from the heat. The residual heat will finish cooking the scallops to perfection.

8. Drain the reserved apple-fennel mixture and discard the lemon halves. In a large salad bowl, toss half of the watercress with the fennel-apple mixture. Add the reserved vinaigrette and ⅛ cup of the hazelnuts and toss gently. Season with salt and pepper.

Vinaigrette

4 shallots, peeled and cut lengthwise into quarters

2 tablespoons olive oil, plus ½ cup

Salt and freshly ground black pepper, to taste

2 sprigs fresh thyme, minced

3 springs fresh rosemary, minced

Juice of 1 orange

Juice and zest of ½ lemon

2 cloves garlic, minced

Salad

8 sea scallops

1 Honeycrisp apple, cored and thinly sliced (or substitute Gala or Jonagold)

2 fennel bulbs, stem trimmed and shaved

Juice of 2 lemons, halves reserved

Salt and freshly ground black pepper, to taste

2 tablespoons grapeseed oil

2 tablespoons unsalted butter

1 bunch watercress, all but ½ inch of the stems removed

⅛ cup hazelnuts, toasted and crushed, plus ⅛ cup for garnish

continued on next page >>>

9. Arrange the salad on 4 salad plates, and top each with 2 scallops. Place the remaining watercress on top and then garnish with the remaining ⅛ cup hazelnuts and serve.

FOR THE **kiddos**

The kids' version of this salad simplifies the mix of flavors a bit, and makes good use of orange and lemon juices. Kids really love anything citrusy, so replacing your usual vinaigrettes with a citrus dressing is a great way to get them to dive into a salad. However, whenever you use lemon, lime or grapefruit in a dressing, add agave nectar or a pinch of sugar to take the edge off for young tongues.

SERVES 4

1 Whisk all the dressing ingredients together in a medium bowl until completely blended.

2 Add the apple and fennel to the dressing and marinate for at least 15 minutes and up to an hour. Taste the dressing and add salt and additional mayonnaise if needed to counteract the licorice flavor of the fennel. Remove the apple and fennel and set aside. Add the romaine to the dressing and toss gently.

3 Melt the butter in a medium skillet over medium-high heat. Panfry the scallops until golden and cooked through, about 5 minutes. Remove the scallops to a plate and cut into half-moons. Pour the lemon juice over the half-moons.

4 Create a silly serpent. Spread the romaine out on 4 individual plates to create the surface of the ocean. Spread the apples (reserving 4 slices) and fennel under the romaine and scatter the almonds as the ocean floor.

5 Place 4 scallop half-moons, cut side down, in a row on the salad's surface on each plate. (This is the body of the serpent as it plunges in and out of the water.) Carve the serpent's head from a piece of the reserved apple. Cut out a mouth and eyes, and you can even use edible markers to draw a face. Stick a piece of watercress in the last scallop half-moon to make a tail, and use a small piece on the head of the serpent.

Dressing

½ cup mayonnaise

Juice of 1 orange

Juice and zest of ½ small lemon

1 tablespoon shallot vinaigrette (from recipe above)

Pinch of granulated sugar (or ½ teaspoon agave nectar)

Mayonnaise (optional)

Salt and freshly ground black pepper, to taste

Salad

2 Honeycrisp apples, cored and cut into 12 pieces each

¼ fennel bulb, stem trimmed and shaved

½ head romaine lettuce, cut into medium-size pieces

1 tablespoon chopped almonds

Scallops

2 tablespoons butter

4 scallops

1 tablespoon freshly squeezed lemon juice

GUMMY BEAR SALAD

Okay, now, just hear me out. I know it sounds strange. But trust me, it's great. This was the very first salad I created as the Gourmet Dad. I wanted my kids to eat more salad, and I asked myself, *What is a universal sweet that kids love, that I could put in a dressing, and that would go nicely with the acidity from the vinegar traditionally found in dressings?* Eureka! Gummy bears. I went to my secret lair and started melting down gummy bears and mixing them with oils and vinegars, and behold! Success! I had invented the perfect kiddie salad dressing (insert evil laugh here). The kids loved it, and better yet, the adults went crazy for it. It reminded them of their childhood. That's what any home cook or chef wants to hear—that they evoked a strong emotion from someone with one of their dishes. That's what it's all about.

30 **gummy bears, plus 12 for garnish**

1 **head butter lettuce**

1 **head romaine lettuce**

1 **tablespoon yellow mustard**

1 **tablespoon apple cider vinegar**

1 **tablespoon orange juice**

Pinch of salt and pepper

¼ **cup grapeseed oil**

SERVES 4

1. Place the gummy bears in a small saucepan and just barely cover with water. Melt the gummies over medium heat, stirring constantly. (Kids just love watching them melt and liquefy.) Once the gummies have completely dissolved, set the saucepan aside and let cool to room temperature.

2. Cut the lettuces into ¼-inch strips. Set aside in a large salad bowl.

3. Combine the gummy liquid, the mustard, vinegar, orange juice, salt and pepper in a blender or food processor. Blend on low until well mixed. Slowly drizzle in the grapeseed oil while blending on low.

4. Taste and adjust the flavor.

5. Place the butter lettuce and the romaine in a large bowl. Drizzle half the dressing over the lettuce and toss to coat. Add more dressing as needed, but don't overdress the salad. Spoon the salad into 4 salad bowls and garnish each with 3 gummy bears by sticking the bears to the side of the salad bowl, just above the salad.

HEIRLOOM TOMATO AND BURRATA SALAD
with Balsamic Cinnamon Reduction

If you haven't tried it before, you're going to flip over burrata. The word is Italian for "buttered," and it's basically a type of mozzarella with cream inside. Kids love it, too. They even love saying it because it's fun on the tongue: "Burrrrata." Like any mozzarella, burrata pairs perfectly with tomatoes. (If you can't find burrata locally, mozzarella pearls or buffalo's milk mozzarella will work just as well in this recipe.) I like to pair this creamy cheese with heirloom tomatoes, because they have so much more flavor, not to mention better color, than the tomatoes you'll find at the supermarket. You can also include some healthy and delicious roasted beets! Toss thick-sliced beets with olive oil, salt and pepper and cook them in a 400°F oven for 20 to 25 minutes, and boom! You just made magic.

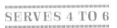

SERVES 4 TO 6

1. Preheat the oven to 375°F.

2. Tear the sourdough into 2-inch cubes. In a large bowl, toss the cubes with the olive oil, salt and pepper. Squeeze each piece to make sure it absorbs the oil. Spread the cubes evenly on a baking sheet and bake until golden brown, about 12 to 15 minutes. Remove the croutons from the oven to a large plate and set aside.

3. Combine the vinegar and the cinnamon stick in a medium heavy pot. Bring to a boil over medium heat. Reduce the heat to medium-low, and reduce the liquid by half, about 10 to 12 minutes. (The liquid should be slightly syrupy, but watch that it doesn't burn or become gummy.) Remove from the heat.

4. Stir the chili powder, brown sugar, salt and pepper into the reduction. Taste and adjust the seasoning if needed. Add a splash of lemon juice to brighten the flavor, if desired. Remove the cinnamon stick and discard. Cool the reduction completely.

5. Combine the reserved croutons, heirloom tomatoes, cherry tomatoes, basil, oregano and olive oil in a large bowl and toss gently. Taste and season with salt and pepper.

6. Place the salad on a serving platter, and arrange the burrata wedges evenly around the salad. Drizzle with the reserved balsamic reduction and garnish with the whole basil leaves before serving.

Croutons

½ loaf sourdough bread, crust removed

¼ cup olive oil

Salt and freshly ground black pepper, to taste

Reduction (sauce)

12 ounces balsamic vinegar

1 cinnamon stick

1 teaspoon ancho chili powder, or to taste

2 teaspoons brown sugar

Salt and freshly ground black pepper, to taste

Splash of freshly squeezed lemon juice (optional)

Salad

1½ pounds heirloom tomatoes, cored and cut into wedges

8 ounces cherry tomatoes, halved

1 small bunch fresh basil, most leaves minced and a few whole for garnish

Minced leaves of 3 sprigs fresh oregano

2 tablespoons olive oil

Salt and freshly cracked black pepper, to taste

8 ounces burrata, cut into wedges

Let it bloom! Transforming salads into flowers gives kids a chance to connect with what they're eating in a fun and satisfying way. It is the best way to re-create a garden on the plate and is the next best thing to picking the vegetables and eating them in the garden.

SERVES 2

1 On a large plate arrange the heirloom tomato wedges so that they resemble flower petals. Build stems using the basil leaves. Create a flowerpot or earthy soil out of the croutons. Next, decorate the middle of each flower with a few pieces of mozzarella.

2 Make little bugs from the cherry tomatoes. Cut the cherry tomatoes in half, arrange them on the plate and attach 2 chive pieces to each to form antennae.

3 In a small bowl, combine the vinegar, olive oil and honey and stir well. Drizzle this dressing over the top of the salad and let your kiddies go to town!

½ pound heirloom tomatoes, cored and cut into wedges

6 small fresh basil leaves

½ cup sourdough croutons (from adult recipe)

3 ounces fresh mozzarella balls or pearls, or whole fresh mozzarella, cut into large cubes

10 cherry tomatoes

2 whole fresh chives, cut into 10 pieces of equal length

2 tablespoons balsamic vinegar

2 tablespoons olive oil

1 teaspoon honey

DEAN'S CRISPY FINGERLING SALAD

Here's a whole new take on potato salad, and one that everyone in the family will love. Anything involving potatoes is kind of a no-brainer for adults, but I look for ways to really make the dish appeal to kids. I've never met a kid who didn't love French fries, so the heart of this salad is, well, fried potatoes. I make the adult version with a sophisticated blend of spices for the potatoes and a really elegant dressing. Switch it up for the kids by giving them a dunking sauce rather than a dressing. Get the kids involved in making this one—you'll quickly learn that they like smashing potatoes almost as much as eating fries.

SERVES 4 TO 6

1. Preheat the oven to 350°F.

2. In a small bowl, combine all the dressing ingredients except the salt and pepper and whisk to blend. Add more water or olive oil if necessary to thin the dressing. Taste and season with salt and pepper. Cover and refrigerate.

3. Toss the potatoes with the olive oil, thyme, sage, salt and pepper. Arrange the potatoes in a single layer on a baking sheet and roast for about 20 minutes, or until fork-tender. Remove the potatoes to a large platter and let cool. When they are cool enough to handle, gently smash each potato so that it is ½ inch thick.

4. Combine the cumin, paprika, salt and pepper in a small bowl and stir well. Set aside.

5. Heat the canola oil in a large skillet over medium-high heat. Fry the potatoes in batches until they are crispy. When all the potatoes are fried, sprinkle them with the reserved cumin seasoning mix. (You can keep the potatoes warm between batches in an oven set to 250°F.)

6. Place the frisée, piquillo peppers and parsley in a large bowl, season with the lemon juice, salt and pepper, and toss. Top the salad with the potatoes and drizzle with the dressing. Serve at once.

Dressing

- 1 cup mayonnaise
- Juice of 1 lemon
- ¼ cup kalamata olives, pitted and diced
- 2 tablespoons olive oil
- 1 tablespoon water
- 2 cloves garlic, peeled and smashed
- ¼ teaspoon cayenne pepper
- Pinch of granulated sugar
- Salt and freshly ground black pepper, to taste

Potatoes

- 3 pounds mixed fingerling potatoes (assorted colors)
- ¼ cup olive oil
- Leaves of 6 sprigs fresh thyme
- Leaves of 2 sprigs fresh sage
- Salt and freshly cracked black pepper, to taste
- 2 teaspoons ground cumin
- 1 teaspoon smoked paprika
- 1 teaspoon salt
- 1 teaspoon freshly ground black pepper
- ½ cup canola oil (or substitute duck fat or bacon fat)

Salad

- 2 heads frisée, torn (or substitute cabbage)
- 2 roasted piquillo peppers, thinly sliced (or substitute 2 roasted medium red bell peppers)
- ¼ cup minced fresh parsley
- Juice of 1 small lemon
- Salt and freshly cracked black pepper, to taste

FOR THE **kiddos**

Be sure to use lots of colored potatoes to keep it fun. For kids, the adventure in eating is as much about appearance as it is about flavor. I've changed the dressing to a dunking sauce, because if there's one thing that all the kids I've met love to do with their food, it's dunk it.

SERVES 4

1 Combine the all dunking sauce ingredients in a small bowl and whisk until well blended.

2 Prepare the potatoes as in the adult recipe, but season with salt only for the little ones. Omit the salad. Serve the potatoes with the dunking sauce.

Buttermilk Dunking Sauce

½ cup mayonnaise

¼ cup sour cream (or substitute crème fraîche)

¼ cup buttermilk

½ clove garlic, minced

Juice of 1 lemon

Salt and freshly ground black pepper, to taste

SHAVED CUCUMBER AND JICAMA SALAD
with Citrus Vinaigrette

This is a refreshing salad that would be right at home on the deck on a hot summer day. It's lively and light, and kids love jicama. (I cut jicama up into sticks for my kids—a great substitute for fries or chips.) The various citrus fruits used in this salad are cut into "supremes" (page 6), creating a salad that is as beautiful as it is tasty.

SERVES 4

1. Prepare the vinaigrette by soaking the shallots in the grapefruit juice in a small bowl for 10 minutes. Add the chili powder, salt and pepper. Slowly whisk in the olive oil until it is fully incorporated. Stir in the cilantro and set aside.

2. Slice the avocado in half and remove the pit and skin. Cut into eighths lengthwise and place the slices in a small bowl. Season the slices with a squeeze of lemon juice to keep them from discoloring and then with salt and pepper.

3. In a large salad bowl, combine the citrus, cucumbers, jicama, watercress and cilantro. Add the vinaigrette and toss to coat.

4. Divide the salad on 4 salad plates. Top each plate with the reserved avocado slices and a sprinkle of walnuts and serve.

Vinaigrette

1 shallot, peeled and finely diced

Juice of 1 grapefruit

¼ teaspoon chili powder, or to taste

Salt and freshly ground black pepper, to taste

½ cup olive oil

1 tablespoon minced fresh cilantro

Salad

2 ripe avocados

Juice of 1 lemon

Salt and freshly cracked black pepper, to taste

1 grapefruit, supremed, juice reserved (see box on page 6)

1 orange, supremed, juice reserved

1 tangelo, supremed, juice reserved

1 Meyer lemon, supremed, juice reserved (substitute tangerines, oranges, other citrus, or even limes to suit preference or availability)

2 English cucumbers, halved, and sliced lengthwise

1 small jicama, peeled and sliced into ⅛-inch-thick strips

1 bunch watercress, all but 1 inch of the stems removed

¼ cup fresh cilantro leaves

¼ cup walnuts, toasted and chopped

Dean's Food 411

Here's another way to make your kids go crazy for citrus. Cut a lemon, a Meyer lemon or an orange into really thin slices on a mandolin, dust each side of the slices with sugar and then grill them. Keep the lemon or orange slices over the flame just long enough so that they soften and caramelize. The little ones go crazy for citrus this way, and you can put it on salads or even ice cream. They also love to watch the process of fruit being grilled.

 FOR THE **kiddos**

The kids' version of this salad has a simpler mix of flavors that won't overwhelm the underage palate.

SERVES 2

1 In a small bowl, combine the orange juice and honey. Slowly drizzle in the olive oil, whisking until entirely blended. Set the vinaigrette aside.

2 Arrange the cucumber slices on 2 salad plates to look like flowing water. Place a lettuce cup on each plate. These will be the lettuce boats.

3 In a medium bowl, toss together the sliced lettuce, avocado, jicama, tangerine segments and orange segments. Toss with vinaigrette. Fill the lettuce cups with the salad mix-

Vinaigrette

Juice of 1 orange

1 tablespoon honey

¼ cup olive oil

Salad

½ cucumber, shaved lengthwise on a mandoline

1 head butter lettuce, sliced into 2-inch pieces (reserve 2 large outer leaves for salad cups)

1 ripe avocado, halved, pit removed, peeled and diced

¼ jicama, cut into long, thick pieces (for flagpoles)

DEAN THE GREEK'S SALAD

Okay, so I'm Scottish, not Greek. But I know a thing or two about putting together a really nice Greek salad (and I make a mean haggis). Because the spices aren't overly hot and I don't go heavy on the vinegar, kids are sure to like this salad every bit as much as adults do.

SERVES 4

1. Combine the tomatoes, cucumbers, red peppers, onions and olives in a large bowl and mix.

2. In a medium bowl, combine the olive oil, vinegar, lemon juice, mustard, sugar, garlic powder, oregano, basil, salt and pepper. Whisk together vigorously until well blended. Taste and add more sugar if the dressing is too acidic.

3. Pour the dressing over the vegetables and olives and toss until well coated. Taste and adjust the seasonings as desired.

4. Serve in individual salad bowls topped with the micro greens and feta cheese.

4 cups cherry tomato halves

2 English cucumbers, diced

1 red bell pepper, diced

1 small red onion, peeled and diced

½ cup black olive halves

½ cup olive oil

5 tablespoons red wine vinegar

Juice of 1 large lemon

1 tablespoon Dijon mustard

1 teaspoon granulated sugar (or more, if desired)

1 teaspoon garlic powder

1 teaspoon dried oregano

1 teaspoon dried basil

1 teaspoon salt

1 teaspoon freshly cracked black pepper

¼ cup micro greens

One 4-ounce package feta cheese, crumbled

SUN-DRIED TOMATO AND WILD ARUGULA SALAD
with Fried Chickpeas and Creamy Dill Dressing

Chickpeas can be used in so many dishes and go so well with just about any flavor, but frying them is the ultimate! Kids have a blast with fried chickpeas, and even though they're fried, the chickpeas retain a lot of beneficial protein, and the rest of the salad contains tons of vitamins, minerals and fiber (that can be our little secret).

SERVES 2

1. Combine all the dressing ingredients in a blender or food processor and blend until smooth. Set aside.

2. Spread the chickpeas on a paper towel–lined plate and gently blot them dry. Heat the canola oil in a medium heavy-duty pot over medium-high heat until it reaches 350°F. Check the temperature of the oil with a cooking thermometer.

3. Once the oil reaches 350°F, fry the chickpeas in batches until golden and crispy, 2½ to 3 minutes. Be especially careful when you add the chickpeas to the pot, as the oil will bubble furiously and will rise in the pot. The chickpeas should remain creamy on the interior but will be golden and crispy on the outside. Remove the chick peas with a skimmer and drain on a paper towel–lined baking sheet. Season with salt. Measure out 1 cup, and eat the rest of the chickpeas as a snack.

4. In a large salad bowl, combine the arugula, radicchio and sun-dried tomatoes and toss with the dressing. Gently fold in 3 ounces of the goat cheese and ¼ cup of the chickpeas.

5. Divide the salad on 2 salad plates. Top each plate with the remaining ¾ cup chickpeas and the remaining 1 ounce goat cheese, and garnish with the dill sprigs.

Dressing

- 2 cups Greek yogurt
- Juice and zest of 1 lemon
- ¼ cup coarsely chopped fresh dill
- 2 tablespoons olive oil
- 1 tablespoon coarsely chopped fresh parsley
- 1 tablespoon coarsely chopped fresh chives
- 1 tablespoon coarsely chopped fresh mint
- Salt and freshly cracked black pepper, to taste

Salad

- One 15-ounce can chickpeas, rinsed and drained
- 3 cups canola oil
- Salt, to taste
- 4 cups wild arugula
- 1 head radicchio, cored and thinly sliced
- 4–6 sun-dried tomatoes, sliced into strips
- 3 ounces goat cheese, crumbled, plus 1 ounce for garnish
- Fresh dill sprigs, stems removed, for garnish

FOR THE kiddos

This is another fun presentation that kids just love. A chickpea, cherry tomato popper with melted cheddar. Kaboom!

SERVES 2

1 Adjust the top rack of the oven so that it is about 6 inches away from the broiler flame.

2 Core each tomato and scoop out the seeds, the best you can.

3 Combine the chickpeas, parsley, mint, ½ cup water and lemon juice in a food processor or blender. Add salt and pepper, and process until smooth.

4 Preheat the broiler to high. Fill each cored tomato with the chickpea puree, arrange in a baking dish and then top each with an equal amount of cheese. Place the tomatoes under the broiler and broil until the cheese has melted. (Use any leftover chickpea puree as a dip for vegetables.)

5 Remove the tomato poppers to a large plate and and let them cool enough for the kids to eat. Top off each tomato with a fried chickpea from the adult recipe.

6 Toss the romaine with the dressing from the adult version and divide between 2 salad plates. Place the tomato poppers atop the romaine and drizzle with yogurt. Serve with a piece of toast if your kids are dippers!

½ pint cherry tomatoes

One 15-ounce can chickpeas, rinsed and drained

1 tablespoon chopped parsley

1 tablespoon chopped mint

½ cup water

Juice of ½ small lemon

Salt and freshly cracked black pepper, to taste

½ cup grated cheddar cheese

2 cups sliced romaine lettuce

¼ cup Greek yogurt

GRILLED CALAMARI, SWEET PEAS AND KALE SALAD *with Chipotle Ranch Dressing*

Kids are more adventurous than most people give them credit for. Take my little guy Liam—he loves calamari. He's even seen it whole, and he'll still eat it. That's why I don't hesitate to keep the calamari in the kids' version of this salad. But I do dial back a bit on the spices and the heat. The adult version includes a lot of appealing smoky flavors and a couple of different kinds of chili peppers, which can overwhelm the young palate.

SERVES 4

1. Process the chipotles in a food processor until smooth. Add the lime juice and zest and the olive oil, and pulse until completely incorporated.

2. Rub the squid with the chipotle marinade, place in a medium bowl, cover and refrigerate for 30 minutes (and no more than 1 hour). Preheat the grill, or a grill pan if cooking indoors, over medium-high heat, while the squid is marinating.

3. In a small bowl, combine all the dressing ingredients and whisk until thoroughly blended. Taste and adjust the seasonings as desired. Set aside.

4. In a large salad bowl, combine the kale, peas and shallots. Toss with the dressing to coat, and season with salt and pepper. Allow the salad to marinate while you are grilling the squid, so that the kale wilts slightly.

5. Coat the bread slices with olive oil, season with salt and pepper, and toast on the grill.

Dean's Food 411

Children's palates just can't handle the spiciness that an adult's can. For instance, the chile de árbol in the adult version of the calamari salad above can be overpowering to kids. I balance it for adults and hold back for the kids to give them just a little taste. Chipotle is the same—all you would ever use for kids is a micro pinch, just so it's there enough to get them a little familiar with the taste but not turn them into fire-breathing dragons.

Calamari
- 2 chipotle peppers in adobo sauce, or to taste
- Juice and zest of 2 limes
- ⅓ cup olive oil
- 8 baby squid bodies, cleaned, rinsed and dried (tentacles are optional)

Dressing
- ½ cup olive oil
- Juice of 2 limes
- 2 tablespoons minced black olives
- 1 tablespoon smoked paprika
- 2 teaspoons honey
- 1 chile de árbol, seeded and very thinly sliced, or to taste
- Salt and freshly cracked black pepper, to taste

Salad
- 1 bunch black kale or Swiss chard, stems removed and very thinly sliced
- 1 cup fresh sweet peas (or substitute frozen, sautéing quickly in 1 tablespoon unsalted butter)
- 1 shallot, peeled and thinly sliced
- Salt and freshly cracked black pepper, to taste
- 1 French baguette, cut into 1-inch-thick slices
- ¼ cup olive oil, plus extra for drizzling

6. Grill the squid, turning it a quarter at a time, to achieve an even char all around, 4 to 5 minutes. Remove to a plate to cool. Once cool, slice 4 of the squid bodies into rings, leaving the remaining 4 squid whole. Add the rings to the salad and toss to coat.

7. Divide the salad between four salad plates, and top each with a whole squid and garnish with a slice of grilled bread. Place the extra grilled bread on a plate or in a basket. Drizzle each salad with olive oil, if desired, and serve with the extra grilled bread.

FOR THE kiddos

You might be surprised at how interested your kids are in the squid. I let my little guys get involved with cutting and preparing the squid, especially breading them. Kids love breading anything because it's a chance to get themselves—and everything else—really messy.

SERVES 4

1 Marinate the squid in the buttermilk for 30 minutes to 1 hour. Mix the bread crumbs and the parsley in a medium bowl. Bread the squid one at a time by letting excess buttermilk drip off a squid and then rolling it in the bread-crumb mixture. Arrange the breaded squid on a plate and set aside. Discard the leftover buttermilk marinade.

2 Heat the oil in a large saucepan with high sides over medium-high heat until it reaches 350°F. Check the temperature of the oil with a cooking thermometer. Fry the squid in 2 batches until golden brown and then remove with a skimmer and drain on a paper towel–lined plate. Be careful. The oil will bubble up, splatter and pop during the frying process. Keep the kids away from the saucepan and the hot calamari.

3 Toss the romaine and the peas in a salad bowl with the buttermilk dunking sauce. Fold in the calamari and serve.

4 squid bodies, cleaned, rinsed, dried and sliced into rings

½ cup buttermilk

½ cup fine, dry bread crumbs

1 tablespoon minced fresh parsley

3 cups canola oil

¼ head romaine lettuce, chopped

½ cup fresh peas

Buttermilk dunking sauce, page 19

My Favorite
STUFFING SALAD

I love bread salads because the flavors blend together so well and they go with just about anything. This stuffing salad combines some of my favorite flavors and is a light take on (and a nice change from) the traditional holiday favorite.

SERVES 4

1. Preheat the oven to 300°F.

2. Heat the oil in a medium skillet over medium heat. Add the sausage and sauté, breaking it up with a wooden spoon as it cooks, until browned and cooked through, about 10 minutes. Drain the sausage and stir in the sage and parsley. Cover and keep warm.

3. Spread the bagel pieces on a baking sheet and toast for 10 minutes. Remove to a large bowl and pour the melted butter over them. Mix thoroughly to ensure the butter is absorbed.

4. Combine the tomatoes, apples, onions, cranberries and sugar in a medium saucepan and cook over low heat, stirring occasionally, until the ingredients soften and the flavors meld, about 10 minutes. Cover and keep warm.

5. Add the sausage, the tomato-apple mixture, spinach and pine nuts to the bagel cubes in the salad bowl. Season with salt and white pepper, toss gently to mix and serve.

1 tablespoon grapeseed oil

¾ pound sweet Italian link sausage, casings removed

2 tablespoons finely minced fresh sage

2 tablespoons finely chopped parsley

4 plain bagels, cut into 1-inch cubes

½ cup unsalted butter, melted

2 cups halved grape tomatoes

2 Granny Smith apples, peeled, cored and diced

1 red onion, peeled and thinly sliced

½ cup dried cranberries

1 teaspoon granulated sugar

5 cups baby spinach

¾ cup pine nuts, toasted

Salt and freshly cracked white pepper, to taste

SWEET CORN AND ROASTED JALAPEÑO SALAD
with Cilantro-Avocado Dressing

Stripping kernels off the cob is a great way to get little kids involved in cooking, and to be honest, I find it kind of fun, too. This is a Mexican-style mix of flavors that would be right at home served under the sun with a pitcher of margaritas and some chilled juice boxes.

SERVES 4

1. Preheat the oven to 400°F.

2. Char the jalapeños, white onion and garlic whole, with their skins on, over the burner of a gas stove set on low. If your stove is electric, place these on a baking sheet and broil them in the oven, rotating them to char all around.

3. Place the charred jalapeños, onion and garlic in a medium bowl, add 1 tablespoon of the vegetable oil, and toss to coat. Transfer to a baking dish. Roast until tender, 25 to 35 minutes. Remove to a plate and let cool.

4. Toss the corn with 1 tablespoon vegetable oil. Spread onto a baking sheet and roast, stirring occasionally, for 15 to 20 minutes. Remove and set aside.

5. Once the jalapeños, onion and garlic are cool enough to handle, remove the charred skins from the onion and garlic. Squeeze out 5 cloves from the head of garlic and set aside. (Reserve the rest for spreads or sauces.)

6. Combine the lime juice, ¾ of the cilantro, the cumin seeds and the scallions in a blender or food processor. Process on low until nearly smooth. Add the avocados and blend just enough to incorporate. Slowly add the olive oil. Add water as necessary to thin the dressing. Taste and season with salt and pepper.

7. Trim the jalapeños and remove the seeds. Chop the charred onion and jalapeños and combine in a large bowl with the roasted garlic. Add the corn, 3 ounces of the cheese, the remaining cilantro (leaves only), tomatoes and mâche.

8. Pour the dressing over the salad and toss to coat. Divide between 4 salad plates and garnish each with a sprinkling of cheese.

4 jalapeño peppers

1 white onion

1 bulb garlic

1 tablespoon vegetable oil, plus 1 tablespoon for the corn

6 ears corn, husked, rinsed and kernels cut off the cob

¼ cup lime juice

1 bunch fresh cilantro, stems removed

2 teaspoon cumin seeds, toasted and ground

4 scallions, root ends removed and coarsely chopped

2 ripe avocados, halved, peeled and pitted

½ cup olive oil

Salt and freshly cracked black pepper, to taste

3 ounces cotija cheese, crumbled, plus 1 ounce for garnish (or substitute queso fresco or feta)

2 cups cherry tomatoes, halved

2 cups mâche (or substitute Bibb lettuce or another butter lettuce)

FOR THE kiddos

Convert this salad into a fresh salsa! This is also a wonderful salad to get kids involved in the kitchen. They can strip the corn off the cob, help you roast the veggies and—if they're old enough—cut up ingredients.

SERVES 4

1. Combine the corn, tomatoes, onions, the ½ cup of olive oil, the lime juice, garlic and cumin in a food processor. Let your child pulse the mixture, pushing the button on and off, until it has the consistency of a chunky salsa. Pour the salsa into a large bowl.

2. Slightly mash the avocado with a fork and add to the salsa. Stir in the cheeses.

3. Heat 1 teaspoon of the remaining olive oil in a large skillet over medium heat and fry a tortilla until light golden. Add the remaining 1 teaspoon oil to the skillet and fry the remaining tortilla. Cut the tortillas into triangles. (They are a healthier alternative to processed and fried tortilla chips.) Serve the salsa with the tortilla triangles for dipping.

Roasted corn kernels from 6 ears of corn (see recipe above)

2 cups cherry tomatoes, chopped

½ roasted white onion, peeled and coarsely chopped (see recipe above)

½ cup olive oil, plus 2 teaspoons

Juice of 1 lime

1 roasted garlic clove, peeled and coarsely chopped (see recipe above)

1 teaspoon ground cumin

1 ripe avocado, halved, peeled and pitted

¼ cup cotija cheese mixed with ¼ cup shredded cheddar cheese

2 large flour tortillas

Chapter two

SOUP GROUP

At the Casa Crazytime, we don't just trot soups out for rainy days and cold winter nights— they're every bit as good in spring and summer. All that abundant fresh produce in the warmer seasons of the year makes for some delicious soup possibilities. I like to take advantage of what's at the local farmers' market, and I'll show you how to turn seasonal produce into great corn chowder, fresh pea soup, tomato garlic soup, and more.

When I was a kid, there were only two soups in my house—my dad's notorious sausage soup and my mom's hearty beef and vegetable soup. I despised them both (the soups, not my parents). My mom's soup wasn't so bad (though once she tried to pull a fast one on me by adding a can of beef stew to her own soup and saying I couldn't complain, because it was my favorite, Chunky Beef from a can!). But that sausage soup? Pure evil.

Fortunately, there are no evil soups in all the recipes that follow. These are some seriously tasty and nutritious dishes, and I will never ask you to try to pull one over on your little ones. Well . . . maybe just a little. They don't really need to know about the onions and the garlic and the cumin and the coriander, do they? They don't need to know that butternut squash is chock-full of vitamins, minerals and fiber. All they need to know is that soup is awesome, and cooking soup can be true kitchen fun.

BUTTERNUT SQUASH SOUP
with Pumpkin-Seed Garnish

This is a hands-down amazing soup. I don't know very many people, or kids, for that matter, who don't like butternut squash soup. It has a silky, rich texture, an alluringly sweet flavor and a gorgeous color. I like to serve it on a regular basis because my kids think it's delicious and they've never caught on that they're eating a ton of vitamins A, B$_6$ and C, and beta-carotene. You practically need a prescription to get that many nutrients in one place! I add a pumpkin-seed garnish that goes perfectly with the flavor of the squash, but I serve the kids a subtler version that goes a bit lighter on the spices. I also may mix in some brown sugar, which really makes it a crowd-pleaser at the kids' table.

SERVES 4 TO 6

1. Preheat the oven to 400°F. Heat two baking sheets in the oven for 2 minutes.

2. In a large mixing bowl, combine the squash, apples, shallots and garlic. Drizzle with the olive oil, season with salt and pepper, and toss to coat. Spread the squash-apple mixture on the preheated baking sheets, scatter the thyme sprigs on top and bake for 30 to 35 minutes, or until the squash is tender. Set aside.

3. In a small pot, heat the stock, agave nectar, ginger and cayenne over medium heat and cook for 5 minutes, stirring frequently.

4. Pour ½ cup of the stock mixture into a blender, and add about ½ cup of the roasted squash and apples. Blend until smooth. Repeat this process with the remaining squash and apples, blending in batches.

5. Pour the blended squash-apple mixture into a large pot and add enough stock to thin it to a soup consistency (you may need 1 to 2 cups of additional stock for this). Stir in the butter. Taste and adjust the seasoning as desired, adding more cayenne for a spicier soup (but keep in mind that the pumpkin-seed garnish has cayenne and black pepper in it).

6. Heat the oil for the pumpkin seed garnish in a medium pot over medium heat. In a small bowl, combine the cayenne, salt, pepper and sugar.

7. When the oil is 350°F, fry the pumpkin seeds until they puff up and brown, 30 to 60 seconds. Remove the pumpkin seeds with a

Soup

2 large butternut squashes, halved lengthwise, seeded, peeled and cut into 1-inch cubes

2 Pink Lady apples, peeled, cored and cut into 1-inch cubes (or substitute Gala)

2 medium shallots, peeled and quartered

3 cloves garlic, peeled

2 tablespoons olive oil

Salt and freshly cracked black pepper, to taste

6 sprigs fresh thyme

4 to 6 cups vegetable stock

2 tablespoons agave nectar (or substitute honey)

One 1-inch piece fresh ginger, peeled and grated

½ teaspoon cayenne pepper

1 tablespoon unsalted butter

½ cup crème fraîche, for garnish

Pumpkin-Seed Garnish

2 cups canola oil

1 teaspoon cayenne pepper

2 teaspoons salt

¼ teaspoon black pepper

½ teaspoon granulated sugar

¼ cup raw shelled pumpkin seeds

skimmer and place them on a paper towel–lined plate.
Once they have cooled slightly, add them to the seasoning mixture
and toss.

8. Ladle the soup into individual bowls and top with the crème fraîche
and pumpkin-seed garnish before serving.

FOR THE kiddos

As with other spicy dishes, you're going to want to pull back on the spices a bit, especially the cayenne, which you can safely drop from the recipe. I also replace the pumpkin-seed garnish with tamer croutons. But the real trick is to tickle kids' fancies with the presentation. Cut the tops off of some mini pumpkins and keep the tops for lids. Then have your kids hollow out the pumpkins using sturdy spoons. When you're ready to serve the soup, use the hollowed-out pumpkins as bowls and top with the simple butter bread cubes. Place a pumpkin lid on the side of each bowl.

Butter Bread Cubes

1 cup ½-inch cubed French bread, crusts removed

3 tablespoons unsalted butter, melted

Salt, to taste

1 Preheat the oven to 350°F.

2 Toss all the ingredients together and squeeze the bread cubes so that they become saturated with the butter. Spread the cubes on a nonstick baking sheet.

3 Bake the bread cubes for 12 to 15 minutes, turning them over halfway through the baking time. The bread cubes should be golden but still soft in the center.

CREAM OF MUSHROOM SOUP
with Herbed Croutons

Cream of mushroom is a soup-pot classic; there's a good reason Campbell's has made their version nonstop since 1934. If something works for you, stick with it. So here's my version, which has worked for me since 1998. The trick? Use a combination of plentiful and easy-to-find cremini mushrooms, also known as brown button mushrooms, along with delicious wild varieties. I use a flavor-rich Mexican chili pepper for some zip and a dose of Dijon mustard. Lastly, no mushroom soup comes out of my kitchen without some handcrafted croutons.

SERVES 4

1. Preheat the oven to 325°F.

2. In a small saucepan over medium heat, combine the butter and olive oil for the croutons and cook until the butter melts. Add the garlic, and then remove the saucepan from the heat and let the garlic steep while the mixture cools.

3. Place the bread cubes in a medium bowl. Stir the oregano, parsley, thyme, salt and pepper into the butter-oil mixture, and then pour it over the bread cubes. Gently move the bread cubes around so that they absorb the herb-butter mixture. Spread the bread cubes on a cookie sheet and bake for 12 to 15 minutes, or until golden brown, turning the cubes over halfway through baking. Set the croutons aside.

4. Prepare the soup by heating the butter and oil in a large, heavy stock-pot over medium heat. Add the onions and sauté until they begin to caramelize, 5 to 10 minutes. Add the scallions, garlic and chile de árbol, and sauté until the garlic is translucent.

5. Increase the heat to medium-high and add the cremini mushrooms, wild mushrooms, thyme and rosemary, and sauté for 5 to 10 minutes, or until the mushrooms begin to break down and release their natural juices.

6. Add the sherry and cook until the liquid is reduced by half. Add the stock and bring to a boil. Reduce the heat and simmer, uncovered, for about 30 minutes. Discard the thyme and rosemary sprigs. Whisk in the heavy cream and mustard, and add salt and pepper.

7. Puree the soup in batches in a blender, or use an immersion blender (or leave it chunky for a rustic-style soup). Return the soup to the stockpot and simmer until it is heated through. Ladle the soup into 4 soup bowls, and garnish with the reserved croutons and the parsley. Serve at once.

Herbed Croutons

- 4 tablespoons unsalted butter
- ¼ cup olive oil
- 1 clove garlic, peeled and finely minced
- 1 loaf challah bread, torn into 1-inch cubes
- 2 tablespoons chopped fresh oregano
- 2 tablespoons chopped fresh parsley
- 1 tablespoon chopped fresh thyme
- Salt and freshly cracked black pepper, to taste

Soup

- 2 tablespoons unsalted butter
- 1 tablespoon olive oil
- 1 yellow onion, peeled and sliced
- 3 scallions, root ends removed and sliced
- 3 cloves garlic, peeled and sliced
- 1 chile de árbol, seeded and sliced (or substitute ½ teaspoon crushed red pepper flakes)
- 1 pound cremini mushrooms, stems trimmed, thinly sliced
- 1 pound wild mushrooms (such as shiitake or maitake), thinly sliced
- 3 sprigs fresh thyme
- 1 sprig fresh rosemary
- ¼ cup dry sherry (or substitute vermouth)
- 5 cups vegetable stock
- ¾ cup heavy cream
- 1½ tablespoons Dijon mustard
- Salt and freshly ground black pepper, to taste
- 2 tablespoons chopped fresh parsley, for garnish

FOR THE kiddos

It always amazes me that kids, who can't get enough of playing in the dirt, balk at seeing identifiable pieces of mushroom floating in their Cream of Mushroom Soup. For kids, this soup should have a uniform texture and color, and a simplified flavor mix. Omit the chile de árbol and the sherry, and swap the Dijon for plain yellow mustard. And, much as I love my Herbed Croutons, the kids are more into neat-looking food than herbal flavor blends. For their version, cut the garlic and herbs in the croutons by half. Instead of cubed croutons, have the kids make shapes out of the challah bread with a cookie cutter. And use sliced white bread instead of challah if your little ones prefer that.

My Mom's
CHICKEN AND DUMPLINGS

My mom was no Julia Child — she'd be the first to admit it. But she did have a few house specialties that rocked. This was one of them. If you've ever had true chicken and dumplings, you know that it's probably the ultimate comfort food, mostly due to the dumplings' texture. My mom's dumplings had a thin, gooey layer on the outside and a pillowy light and dry interior. However, dumplings are not necessarily the same North to South. Ask someone below the Mason-Dixon Line — or a French Canadian — and they'll want more of a noodle. Mine are the more traditional Northern (and Canadian) version, puffy little balls of doughy heaven. A hint of mint adds an unusual and appealing edge. Make bite-size dumplings for the kiddos — I haven't met a kid who doesn't love chicken and dumplings!

SERVES 4 TO 6

1. Preheat the oven to 400°F.

2. Place the chicken in a large shallow baking dish, season the chicken with the salt and pepper, and rub all over with the mustard. Let the chicken sit for at least 30 minutes at room temperature so that the flavors penetrate.

3. Heat the oil in a heavy stockpot over medium-high heat. Add the chicken, skin side down, and sear it until it is golden brown. You will need to do this in batches. Turn the heat off but leave the pot on the burner.

4. Transfer the browned chicken pieces to a baking sheet, and bake for 20 to 25 minutes, or until an instant-read thermometer reads 160°F when stuck in a fleshy part of the chicken. Remove the chicken and set aside to cool.

5. While the chicken cools, make the dumpling batter. In a medium bowl, whisk together the flour, parsley, mint, oregano, baking powder, salt and pepper until well mixed.

6. Combine the milk and butter in a medium saucepan and cook over medium-high heat until the butter melts. Stir this mixture into the dry ingredients, and then stir in the soda water. The batter will be sticky. Cover and refrigerate while you prepare the sauce and shred the chicken.

continued on next page >>>

Chicken

3 pounds chicken breasts and thighs, skin on and bone in, trimmed of excess fat

1½ teaspoons salt

1 teaspoon freshly ground black pepper

2 tablespoons coarse mustard

1 tablespoon canola oil

Dumplings

2 cups all-purpose flour

2 teaspoons chopped fresh parsley

2 teaspoons chopped fresh mint

2 teaspoons minced fresh oregano

1½ teaspoons baking powder

¼ teaspoon salt

¼ teaspoon freshly ground black pepper

¼ cup whole milk

1½ tablespoons butter

½ cup soda water

Sauce

¼ cup dry sherry

2 tablespoons butter

3 carrots, peeled and diced

2 celery stalks, diced

1 yellow onion, peeled and diced

½ cup chopped cremini mushrooms

2 cloves garlic, peeled and finely minced

2 tablespoons chopped fresh thyme

7. For the sauce, heat the stockpot that you used for the chicken over medium heat. Add the sherry, scrape up any brown bits on the bottom of the stockpot, and simmer until the liquid is reduced by half.

8. Add the butter and carrots and sauté for about a minute. Add the celery and sauté for another minute. Add the onions, mushrooms, garlic and thyme, and cook for about 8 minutes, or until the vegetables are almost tender.

9. Sprinkle the flour over the vegetables in the stockpot and stir to make a paste. Slowly add the chicken stock, whisking as you go to prevent lumps from forming. Bring the sauce to a boil and then reduce the heat and simmer while cutting the reserved chicken. Dice the cooked chicken, discarding the skin and bones. Add the chicken to the sauce, along with the peas. Season the stew with salt and pepper and return to a simmer.

10. Using a spoon, form balls 1 inch in diameter from the dumpling batter. Drop the balls into the simmering stew, leaving space around each, as they will expand. Cook, covered, for 15 minutes, or until the dumplings are firm and fluffy.

11. Stir in the lemon juice, garnish with parsley and serve.

¼ cup all-purpose flour

5 cups chicken stock

1 cup fresh peas, blanched (or use frozen)

Juice of ½ lemon

½ cup minced fresh parsley, for garnish

Dean's
ITALIAN WEDDING SOUP

I may not be Italian, but I often play one in my kitchen. One of my favorite ways to channel my inner Deanissimo is with this soup. Legend has it that the name is a mistranslation of the Italian for "married soup," what the original version was called because all the ingredients blended so well together. Doesn't matter. I'd serve it at a wedding, a birthday or even a bar mitzvah! The meatballs are the heart of the soup, and you can even make them to accompany pasta or just to eat by themselves. But this soup recipe with these meatballs is a marriage made in heaven.

SERVES 4 TO 6

1. Preheat the oven to 375°F. Coat a baking sheet with the olive oil.

2. In a large mixing bowl, combine the Parmigiano-Reggiano, bread crumbs, egg, parsley, oregano, tomato paste, garlic, fennel seed, salt and pepper and mix thoroughly. Mix in the beef and pork with your hands and knead until the mixture has a uniform consistency. (This step is the perfect chance to get the little ones involved. They'll love getting their hands dirty!)

3. Form the meat mixture into 1-inch meatballs and place them about 1 inch apart on the prepared baking sheet. Bake the meatballs for 15 to 20 minutes, or until they are cooked through. Remove from the oven and set aside.

4. Prepare the soup. Heat the olive oil in a large stockpot over medium-high heat, add the onions, carrots and celery, and sauté for 5 minutes.

5. Add the red pepper flakes, salt and pepper. Add the kale and stir until it has wilted, about 7 minutes. Add the garlic and cook for 1 minute.

6. Add the chicken stock and bring to a boil. Reduce the heat to medium and add the meatballs and the oregano. Simmer the soup for 10 to 12 minutes, or until the meatballs are heated through.

7. Just before serving, stir in the lemon juice and zest and the parsley. Taste and add salt and pepper as desired. Serve the soup in warmed soup bowls and garnish with the shaved Parmesan.

Meatballs

Olive oil, for greasing the baking sheet

½ cup finely grated Parmigiano-Reggiano

¼ cup panko bread crumbs

1 large egg

2 tablespoons chopped fresh parsley

1 tablespoon chopped fresh oregano

1 tablespoon tomato paste

2 small cloves garlic, peeled and crushed

1 teaspoon toasted and ground fennel seed

Salt and freshly ground black pepper, to taste

½ pound beef chuck, ground fresh

½ pound pork loin, ground fresh

Soup Base

1 tablespoon olive oil

1 yellow onion, peeled and diced

½ cup diced carrots

½ cup diced celery

½ teaspoon crushed red pepper flakes

½ teaspoon salt

½ teaspoon fresh ground black pepper

10 cups shredded kale (no stems)

2 cloves garlic, peeled and minced

12 cups chicken stock

1 tablespoon minced fresh oregano

Juice and zest of 1 lemon

1 tablespoon chopped fresh parsley

Shaved Parmesan cheese, for garnish

FOR THE **kiddos**

Eliminate half the herbs and spices in the meatballs and the soup base, and try this fun garnish in place of the shaved Parmesan garnish in the adult version. You'll need a wedding ring or a wedding cake cookie cutter (or a heart or circle cutter if you can't find either of those).

Four 1-inch-thick slices French bread

1 tablespoon softened butter

1 tablespoon olive oil

¼ cup grated Parmesan cheese

1 Use a cookie cutter to cut each slice of bread into a wedding ring, wedding cake, heart or circle shape.

2 Adjust the top rack of the oven so that it is about 6 inches away from the broiler flame. Preheat the broiler on high.

3 Blend the butter and olive oil together in a small bowl or ramekin. Brush each bread shape with the butter-oil spread, arrange on a baking sheet, and toast under the broiler (watch carefully!) until golden. Remove the bread shapes from the oven, top each one with the cheese and broil until the cheese melts. Serve the bread shapes

Spicy
CORN AND CRAB CHOWDER

It's hard to top a chunky chowder for a filling meal in a bowl. Seafood chowders are some of the best (what would New England be without clam chowder?), but add some veggies to the seafood and bang! A major hit that serves up perfectly whenever you need to shake the cold out of your bones. A chowder is essentially a cross between a soup and a stew—and, man, what a cross. In the McDermott house, we like our chowders year-round. That's why I include seasonal fresh corn on the cob in this terrific version, making it the ideal summer meal. I roast the corn to give the soup a really nice grilled sweetness. But like all chowders, this version is perfect for taking the edge off a chilly day, too. Either way, your tongue is going to do a happy dance when it gets a taste of the spice and herb blends in this dish. (I can't believe I just wrote *happy dance*.) One suggestion, though: Buy loose lump crabmeat as fresh as you can get it. Canned crabmeat doesn't really cut it where flavor is concerned.

SERVES 4

- 6 tablespoons olive oil, divided
- 3 medium Yukon Gold potatoes, finely diced
- 1 red bell pepper, seeded and diced
- 1 yellow bell pepper, seeded and diced
- ½ yellow onion, peeled and diced
- 2 cloves garlic, peeled and minced
- 4 cups chicken stock
- ½ bunch fresh cilantro, minced
- 1 chipotle pepper in adobo sauce, seeded and finely minced
- ½ serrano chili pepper, seeded and minced
- 4 cups corn kernels, stripped fresh off the cob
- 2 tablespoons fresh thyme
- 6 ounces jumbo lump crabmeat, divided (2 ounces reserved for garnish)
- ½ teaspoon cayenne pepper
- 2 tablespoons chopped fresh parsley
- 1 tablespoon chopped fresh chives
- Juice of 1 lime
- Salt and freshly ground black pepper, to taste

1. Heat 2 tablespoons of the olive oil in a 6-quart (or larger) pot over high heat. Add the potatoes and sauté just until they are crispy on the outside (this will ensure they don't fall apart in the chowder), 3 to 5 minutes.

2. Reduce the heat to medium, add 1 tablespoon olive oil and the bell peppers, and sauté for 1 minute. Then add the onions and garlic and cook for 2 minutes, or until tender.

3. Pour the chicken stock into the pot and add the cilantro, the chipotle pepper and the serrano chili pepper. Bring to a boil and then reduce the heat to medium-low and simmer.

4. Heat 1 tablespoon olive oil in a large sauté pan over high heat. Sauté the corn in two batches, until golden (be careful because it will spit and spatter). Add the corn to the pot as each batch is cooked. Then add the thyme.

5. Stir in the crab meat right before you're ready to serve the chowder, just so it gets warmed through.

6. In a small mixing bowl, combine the cayenne, parsley and chives with the reserved crab and lime juice. Add in 2 tablespoons of olive oil. Taste and adjust the seasonings as desired. Serve the soup in bowls with a small spoon of the crab mixture as garnish.

FOR THE kiddos

I don't usually take my cooking inspiration from cartoons, but who can deny the culinary expertise of a certain yellow sponge that lives underwater? When I make this chowder for the McDermott brood, I leave the crab out of the chowder and make mini Crabby Patties instead. I also pull back on the spices quite a bit and allow the roasted corn flavor to come through.

SERVES 2 TO 3

1 Thoroughly mix together the crabmeat, bread crumbs, mayonnaise, lemon juice and parsley in a medium bowl. Have the little ones wash their hands and then dive into the mix, rolling out tablespoon-size balls, gently flattening them (if they are patties) and placing them on a plate.

2 Heat the butter and the oil in a large pan over medium-high heat, and until the butter melts. Fry the patties or balls, turning them once, until they are browned all over. Remove them to a paper towel–lined plate and let cool slightly to allow them to firm up.

3 Slide each patty or ball onto its own skewer and serve alongside a small cup of the chowder.

Crabby Patties (or Balls!)

6 ounces lump crabmeat

¼ cup panko bread crumbs

2 tablespoons mayonnaise

1 tablespoon lemon juice

1 teaspoon minced fresh parsley

2 tablespoons unsalted butter

2 tablespoons canola oil

FOR THE **kiddos**

Eliminate the black pepper in the tuiles, using only
Parmesan. Let your kids pick out a favorite large cookie cutter
(I like using a dinosaur cutter). When shaping the Parmesan cheese
on the baking sheet, have the kids tamp down the cheese inside
their cutters to about ⅛ inch thick. Bake the tuiles as described.
Serve them with the soup, but make sure you reduce the amount of
crushed red pepper flakes and cayenne pepper in the soup to just
a pinch of each.

TOMATO-GARLIC SOUP
with Parmesan Tuiles

You might think of tomato as the plainest of soups, but I've given mine a little extra charge with some garlic and cayenne, and use Parmesan tuiles as garnish. A tuile is a thin, brittle cookie served with ice cream, but you can pretty much make a tuile out of anything that can melt and harden. They make ideal garnishes, and the Parmesan tuiles are basically the bling for this soup. This dish is easy to make and special to serve.

SERVES 4

1. Preheat the oven to 400°F. Line a baking sheet with a nonstick baking mat, such as a Silpat, or with aluminum foil.

2. In a small mixing bowl, toss together the Parmesan cheese and black pepper. On the baking sheet, form the cheese mixture into strips 2 inches wide and 4 inches long.

3. Bake in the oven for 5 to 7 minutes, or until golden brown. Remove from the oven, let cool for a minute and then gently lift the tuiles off the baking sheet with a flexible metal spatula. Transfer the tuiles to a wire rack and allow them to cool completely.

4. Reduce the oven temperature to 350°F.

5. Place the head of garlic on a piece of aluminum foil large enough to wrap it in completely. Season with salt and pepper and drizzle with the 1 tablespoon of olive oil. Wrap the garlic tightly in the foil, and roast for 25 to 30 minutes, or until it is golden brown and the garlic begins to ooze out the top. Unwrap the garlic and set it aside to cool.

6. Heat the remaining 1 teaspoon olive oil in a medium stockpot over medium-high heat. Add the onions and cook until they begin to sweat, about 3 minutes. Reduce the heat to medium-low and cook, stirring frequently, until the onions caramelize, about 10 minutes.

7. Add the red pepper flakes and cayenne pepper. Squeeze the roasted garlic from the head and add it to the onions. Add the tomatoes and the minced basil, and season with salt and pepper. Bring to a simmer and cook, covered, for about 30 minutes.

8. Mash the contents of the stockpot with a potato masher into 4 individual bowls. Garnish each with a tuile and a basil leaf and serve.

Tuiles

- 1 cup freshly grated Parmesan cheese

- 1 teaspoon freshly cracked black pepper

Soup

- 1 head garlic, top (point) sliced off

  Salt and freshly ground black pepper, to taste

- 1 tablespoon olive oil, plus 1 teaspoon for sautéing

- 1 yellow onion, peeled and sliced

- ½ teaspoon crushed red pepper flakes, or to taste

- ¼ teaspoon cayenne pepper

  Two 28-ounce cans whole tomatoes

- 1 bunch fresh basil, most leaves minced and 4 left whole for garnish

BEEF SHORT RIB AND VEGETABLE SOUP

All short ribs need is the right amount of cooking—essentially a long bath in a warm sauce—and they become delectable. And what better place for short ribs than in a soup where they can enjoy a long, leisurely soak? The balance of vegetables to that beefy goodness is just about perfect in this soup. And short ribs are like sponges, picking up the soup's heavier, stronger flavors, some of which are provided by my favorite beer. Add a fun garnish, like the Crispy Tater Chips here, and you have a spectacular, filling and flavorful soup that shows off the underappreciated short rib in all its glory.

SERVES 4

1. Remove the short ribs from the refrigerator 30 to 45 minutes before you're ready to cook them. Place the short ribs in a large bowl, season with a good amount of salt and pepper, drizzle with olive oil and toss to coat. (At room temperature the short ribs cook more evenly, and seasonings penetrate the meat more efficiently.)

2. Heat a Dutch oven or a large, heavy soup pot over medium-high heat. Sear the short ribs in batches, turning each piece as it cooks. Be patient and allow the meat to caramelize on all sides. Remove each finished batch of short ribs to a baking sheet.

3. Add the onions and 1 cup of the beer to the Dutch oven. Bring to a boil, and then reduce the heat to medium and cook the onions for 8 minutes, stirring to scrape up any bits stuck to the bottom. Next, add the garlic and cook for 3 minutes. Stir in the tomato jam.

4. Return the short ribs and any accumulated juices to the Dutch oven and add the remaining beer. Cook, stirring occasionally, until the liquid is reduced by half.

Soup

3 pounds boneless beef short ribs, any excess fat trimmed and cut into 2-inch pieces

Salt and freshly cracked black pepper, to taste

2 tablespoons olive oil

2 yellow onions, peeled and sliced

One 12-ounce bottle dark, hearty stout, divided (I recommend Guinness)

4 cloves garlic, peeled and sliced

¼ cup tomato jam or tomato paste

4 cups beef stock

4 sprigs fresh thyme

1 chile de árbol (or substitute ½ to 1 teaspoon crushed red pepper flakes)

5 medium carrots, peeled and diced

4 Yukon Gold potatoes, diced

4 celery stalks, diced

2 parsnips, peeled and diced

½ pound cremini mushrooms, stems removed and mushrooms quartered

Crispy Tater Chips

2 tablespoons finely grated Parmesan cheese

½ teaspoon kosher salt

⅛ to ¼ teaspoon cayenne pepper

⅛ teaspoon freshly ground black pepper

2 cups canola oil

3 fingerling potatoes, sliced paper-thin lengthwise

Dean's Food 411

I like a cold brewski as much as the next guy, but alcoholic beverages in the dishes I cook are there for the flavor, not the kick. That's why, generally, whenever you add beer or another adult beverage to a sauce, you reduce the sauce, thickening it by evaporation. This cooks out much of the alcohol, leaving only the flavor components. If you've ever seen a chef "flame up" a pan to deglaze it while sautéing, they are using the flame from the gas range to quickly burn off the alcohol, rather than letting it evaporate in a longer cooking process.

5. Add the beef stock, the sprigs of thyme and the chile de árbol, and bring to a boil. Then reduce the heat to low, cover, and simmer the meat for about 2 hours, or until it is fork-tender but not falling apart.

6. Add the carrots, potatoes, celery, parsnips and mushrooms. Bring to a boil over medium heat, and then reduce the heat and simmer, covered, for 25 minutes, or until the vegetables are tender. Remove the chile de árbol and thyme sprigs and discard.

7. While the soup cooks, prepare the chips. In a small bowl, mix together the Parmesan, salt, cayenne pepper and black pepper. Set aside.

8. Heat the canola oil in a medium saucepan until it reaches 325°F. Fry the potato slices in the oil in batches until crispy. Remove to a paper towel–lined plate and dust with the seasoning mix.

9. Ladle the soup into 4 soup bowls and serve the Crispy Tater Chips alongside.

FOR THE kiddos

Sometimes "hearty" can be too hearty for young tongues and stomachs. That's why I remove the short ribs in this recipe when they are fork-tender, reserving 1 or more per child. Skewer each piece and set aside. Go ahead and cook the soup as with the adult version, but reheat the skewered meat for about 10 minutes before serving by plunging it in the pot of hot soup. Make the Crispy Tater Chips as described in the recipe, but eliminate the spices and season only with salt. Serve the soup with a handful of the Crispy Tater Chips on the side.

Lemony
POTATO AND HAM SOUP

This soup mixes the hearty, soul-satisfying flavor of ham (and a little bacon) with the bright and sharp flavor of lemon. Throw in a blend of spices and a big helping of potatoes, and you have a winner for any night of the week. Plus, if my Liam is any indication, kids will flip over the chance to whip up a batch of homemade buttermilk. This recipe doesn't need any changes for the kiddos, but I like to cut out pig shapes from pieces of ham. Pigs in slop!

SERVES 4

1. Set the cooked bacon aside for the garnish. In a large, heavy pot, heat the reserved bacon fat and the butter over medium heat. Add the leeks, the ¼ cup of scallions and the garlic, and sauté until tender. Add the potatoes and cook for 5 minutes.

2. Sprinkle the flour over the vegetables. Gradually pour in the stock, stirring vigorously to avoid creating lumps. Add the thyme, nutmeg, salt and pepper. Bring to a boil, and then reduce the heat and simmer, covered, for 15 to 20 minutes, or until the potatoes are tender.

3. Meanwhile, have the kids make the buttermilk by combining the milk and lemon juice in a small bowl and stirring to thoroughly mix. Let sit for 10 to 15 minutes to allow it to curdle.

4. Once the potatoes are tender, blend half the soup solids with the buttermilk in a blender. Pour the mixture back into the pot, add the ham and bring to a simmer. (Avoid bringing the soup to a boil after adding the buttermilk, as the liquid can separate if heated too aggressively.)

5. To make the garnish, season both sides of each lemon slice with salt, pepper and a sprinkle of sugar. Heat a grill pan over high heat. Place the lemon slices in the pan, and sear and caramelize each slice. Rotate and flip them to achieve an even color.

6. Taste the soup and add salt and pepper as desired. Ladle the soup into 4 soup bowls and garnish with the reserved bacon and the remaining 2 tablespoons scallions. Top with the grilled lemon slices and serve.

Soup

- 4 slices thick-cut bacon, cooked, crumbled and 1 tablespoon fat reserved
- 4 tablespoons unsalted butter
- 1 leek (white part only), root end trimmed, washed thoroughly and finely diced
- ¼ cup thinly sliced scallions, plus 2 tablespoons for garnish
- 1 clove garlic, peeled and minced
- 4 cups diced Yukon Gold potatoes
- 4 tablespoons all-purpose flour
- 3 cups chicken stock
- 2 tablespoons minced fresh thyme
- ¼ teaspoon freshly grated nutmeg
- Salt and freshly ground black pepper, to taste
- 1 cup whole milk
- Juice of 2 lemons
- ½ pound cooked ham, skin removed, fat trimmed and cut into ½-inch cubes

Sour-Patch Grilled Lemon Slices

- 2 lemons, seeds removed and cut into ¼-inch slices
- Pinch of salt
- Pinch of freshly ground black pepper
- 1 tablespoon granulated sugar

Not My Dad's
SAUSAGE SOUP

It's amazing that I like food at all after suffering the cruel fate of my father's version of sausage soup. I'm not convinced dishwater wasn't involved. I came up with this spicy recipe just to remind myself that sausage can actually work—and work well—in a soup, especially if you use two different types *and* a heady, full-bodied broth, courtesy of a little whiskey. (Always remember to reduce by half to ensure that the alcohol is entirely cooked off!) This is a soup that eats like a stew, and it is a great choice for a roll-up-your-sleeves, casual get-together with friends.

SERVES 4

1. Brown the Italian sausage in a large pot over medium heat until it is nearly crisp, about 10 minutes. Break up the larger pieces as it cooks. Remove and set aside. Add the butter to the pot and brown the chicken sausage, about 8 minutes. Remove and set aside.

2. Add the carrots, onions and garlic to the pot, and sauté until tender, about 8 minutes. Add the whiskey and scrape up any bits from the bottom of the pot. Cook until the liquid is reduced by half.

3. Mash ¼ cup of the cannellini beans and add them to the pot. Add the sausages, chicken stock, tomatoes, cabbage, mustard, salt and pepper. Bring to a boil, and then reduce the heat and simmer, uncovered, for about 30 minutes. Stir in the remaining whole cannellini beans and continue cooking for another 15 minutes.

4. Meanwhile, prepare the toast garnish. Preheat the broiler on high. Spread butter on each rye bread slice and then season each with salt and pepper. Arrange the slices on a baking sheet and toast under the broiler until they are crispy. Remove from the oven, slather mustard evenly across each slice and top with cheese. Broil very briefly, just until the cheese melts. Remove the rye bread slices to a plate, top with chives and cut diagonally.

5. Ladle the soup into 4 soup bowls and serve with 2 pieces of toast garnish alongside each bowl.

Soup

8 ounces spicy Italian link sausage, casings removed

2 tablespoons unsalted butter

4 ounces chicken link sausage, sliced into ¼-inch rounds

3 carrots, peeled and finely diced

2 yellow onions, peeled and finely diced

2 cloves garlic, peeled and minced

½ cup Irish whiskey

One 15-ounce can cannellini beans, rinsed and drained

10 cups chicken stock

One 28-ounce can diced tomatoes, drained

¼ head green cabbage, shredded

¼ cup spicy beer mustard

Salt and freshly cracked black pepper, to taste

Toast Garnish

2 tablespoons unsalted butter, softened

4 slices rye bread

Salt and freshly cracked black pepper, to taste

4 teaspoons whole-grain mustard

⅓ cup finely grated aged cheddar cheese

1 tablespoon chopped fresh chives

Chapter three

FEATHERS

When I was growing up, I was a little gun-shy of chicken. It was either a big hit or a big miss in my house, and when it missed, it really missed. Some nights it was as dry as a bone, and others it was so undercooked, it was just about rare. In my mom's defense, cooking chicken to perfection can be a little tricky, but it's certainly nothing you can't master with a bit of attention to time and temperature.

And it's a skill well worth mastering, because chicken can be a parent's best friend. Whenever Hattie or Finn or Stella or any one of my little ones has gone on a finicky eating streak, they'll still always eat chicken. What parent hasn't been saved at one time or another by the well-timed chicken nugget or tender? And if there's one word that describes this food, it's *adaptable*. Stir-fry it, sauté it, grill it or even steam it. If you're lucky, if you're that rare parent, your child will go for chicken grilled or sautéed. More likely, the kids just want it with some sort of coating, but let's try to change that!

Chicken picks up flavor like nobody's business. You can pair chicken with curry, lemon, thyme, teriyaki marinade, berries, prunes, you name it. It works with a light sauce or a heavy glaze, and it goes with just about any side dish you can name, making it a great choice for adults, but especially for kids.

And it's budget-friendly food, which means you can experiment in the kitchen without risking a lot. Think of it as your own personal food canvas. All the recipes that follow are products of my own creative culinary exploration, and they include some interesting ways of working with chicken (and working with kids), including searing it with bricks and pounding the heck out of it.

Dean's Food 411

Cooking chicken to the correct temperature is not something you should leave to guesswork. I highly recommend that you have an instant-read thermometer in your arsenal. It will give you peace of mind knowing that your bird is cooked correctly, and it works with meat and pork, too. For chicken, follow the USDA recommendations: Cook whole chicken and chicken pieces, such as breasts and thighs, to 165°F, allowing a 3-minute rest after cooking (the chicken keeps cooking during this period). Ground chicken (and ground turkey, too) should be cooked to 160°F, but no rest is required. When I fry chicken, I cook it until it reaches 155°F, and then I let it sit for at least 5 minutes. The chicken's internal temperature will increase over that time.

Dean's Brick House
LEMON-ROSEMARY CHICKEN

Time to get a little rustic! This dish re-creates some of the magic of cooking in a country brick oven, with the help of a couple of bricks and a handy charcoal grill. I'd suggest, for presentation purposes, if nothing else, that you buy a couple of bricks and dedicate them to cooking and cooking only (you'd be surprised how useful they can be). Otherwise, you can grab a couple of bricks from the garden, thoroughly clean them off and wrap them well in aluminum foil. Grilling with bricks is a great way to make sure the heat is evenly distributed, but it's also a lot of fun to watch the kids' faces when you plunk the bricks down on top of their dinner. The first time Liam saw me do it, he blurted out, "A brick?" in utter shock. "Did that come off the house?" The dish itself is hearty fare, just right for sit-down Sunday dinners with the entire family. Or if you have a smaller crowd, look forward to using the leftovers for wraps, sandwiches, soups or pastas.

SERVES 6

1. Wrap 4 bricks in aluminum foil.

2. Rinse the chickens, remove everything from the cavities and discard. Pat the chickens dry inside and out.

3. Butterfly the chickens. First, cut along both sides of the spine of one of the chickens with a pair of kitchen shears. Remove the spine and discard (or save for stock). Locate the small V-shaped bone between the breasts and make a small slit with a paring knife, just cutting the top of the bone. Lift the chicken up, holding both breasts, and crack outward to almost snap the breastbone.

4. Place the chicken, rib side down, on a cutting board and press into the breasts with the heels of your hands just enough to flatten the chicken. Repeat the butterflying process with the second chicken. Place each butterflied chicken in its own roasting pan. (You can also use two resealable bags.)

5. In a blender, puree all the marinade ingredients, except the salt and pepper, until smooth. Pour the marinade over the chickens and rub on all sides. Refrigerate the chickens, covered, for at least 1 hour and up to 12 hours.

6. Once the chickens have marinated, oil the grill grate. Prepare a charcoal grill, letting the fire burn until the coals are medium hot.

continued on next page >>>

Chicken
Two whole chickens
(3 to 3½ pounds)

Marinade
Juice and zest of 4 lemons

½ cup fresh minced rosemary

¼ cup olive oil

4 cloves garlic, peeled

2 tablespoons fresh oregano

1 shallot, peeled and
coarsely chopped

2 teaspoons smoked paprika

Salt and freshly cracked
black pepper, to taste

Grilled Lemons
5 lemons, ends slightly
trimmed and halved

1 teaspoon salt

1 teaspoon pepper

½ teaspoon granulated sugar

1 tablespoon olive oil

Leaves from 3 sprigs
fresh rosemary

(You can use a gas grill if you don't have a charcoal unit, but the flavor will be better with charcoal.) While the grill is heating up, remove the chickens from the refrigerator. Let the excess marinade drain off and let the chickens come to room temperature. Season with salt and pepper. Discard the marinade.

7. Place the chickens, skin side down, on the grate and then place two bricks atop each chicken, one per breast. Close the grill lid and cook for about 15 minutes.

8. Carefully remove the bricks, flip the chickens and replace the bricks. Continue grilling the chickens for 20 to 25 minutes, or until the juices from the thighs run clear and the internal temperate reaches 165°F. Remove the chickens from the grill to clean platters and let them rest, loosely covered with foil, for 15 minutes. Leave the bricks on the grill.

9. Meanwhile, season the cut side of each lemon half with the salt, pepper and sugar. Drizzle olive oil over the lemon halves and place them cut side down on the grill.

10. Grill the lemon halves for 5 minutes, rotating them a couple of times to achieve an even color. Sprinkle the rosemary over the lemons and continue grilling until charred and softened, 5 to 10 minutes.

11. When serving the chickens, place two of the heated bricks on a heat-proof serving platter (or use two platters, with a single brick on each), drape the chickens over top, and serve with the lemons alongside.

BEAT-UP CHICKEN
in Mushroom Gravy

Dinnertime at the McDermott Asylum often involves a competition between Liam and Hattie, whose definition of helping Dad cook involves running around the kitchen island, screaming at the top of their lungs. Pounding the chicken for this dish is just about an ideal outlet for all that excess energy. Plus, get them working on the chicken and it will be easy to transition them to other, somewhat calmer tasks in the kitchen. I use both thighs and breasts in this dish because the thighs are full of flavor. But if your family prefers breasts, simply double the chicken breast amount. It's also easy to strain the gravy for anyone in the crowd who's not a fan of mushrooms.

SERVES 4

1. Preheat the oven to 375°F. Line a baking sheet with parchment paper.

2. Lay the prosciutto on the prepared baking sheet. Bake until crisp, about 15 minutes. Remove to a plate and set aside. Reduce the oven temperature to 200°F.

3. Cover the surface of a large cutting board with a sheet of plastic wrap. Lay two pieces of chicken, spaced evenly apart, on the cutting board. Top the chicken with another sheet or two of plastic wrap (thick waxed paper will work as well).

4. Use a kitchen mallet with a smooth side (or the bottom of a heavy saucepan) to pound the chicken into cutlets ¼ inch thick. Use glancing blows to keep the chicken from tearing. Remove the chicken to a plate and repeat until all the chicken has been pounded.

5. In a small, shallow bowl, thoroughly mix together the flour, thyme, garlic powder, onion powder, cayenne pepper, salt and pepper. In a separate small bowl, whisk the eggs and 1 teaspoon water, and then add a dash of salt and pepper. In a third small bowl, combine the bread crumbs with a pinch each of salt and pepper.

6. Set the 3 bowls next to each other in the order given above. Dip each piece of chicken in the flour mixture, shake off the excess and then dunk the chicken in the egg. Next, lightly press the chicken down into the bread crumbs. Place the chicken cutlet on a wire rack and repeat until all the chicken is breaded. Set the wire rack with

continued on next page ⟩⟩⟩

Beat-Up Chicken

- 6 slices prosciutto

- 4 boneless, skinless chicken thighs, any excess fat trimmed

- 2 boneless, skinless chicken breasts, halved crosswise and any excess fat trimmed

- ½ cup all-purpose flour

- 1 tablespoon finely minced fresh thyme

- ½ teaspoon garlic powder

- ½ teaspoon onion powder

- ¼ teaspoon cayenne pepper

- 1 teaspoon salt, plus more to season

- ¼ teaspoon black pepper, plus more to season

- 3 large eggs

- 2 cups fine bread crumbs

- 4 cups Crisco shortening or oil

Mushroom Gravy

- 2 tablespoons bacon fat (or substitute canola oil)

- ¾ pound cremini mushrooms, stems trimmed and mushrooms sliced

- ½ pound white button mushrooms, stems trimmed and mushrooms sliced

- ¼ pound shiitake mushrooms, stems removed and caps sliced

- 1 shallot, peeled and finely chopped

- 1 tablespoon fresh thyme

- 3 tablespoons all-purpose flour

- 2 tablespoons Madeira wine

- 1½ cups chicken stock

the chicken cutlets on a baking sheet and refrigerate the cutlets for at least 20 minutes.

7. In a large cast-iron skillet with at least 2-inch sides, heat the Crisco over medium heat to 350°F.

8. Remove the chicken cutlets from the refrigerator and gently slide 2 cutlets into the skillet. Fry for 3 to 5 minutes, or until golden brown on the bottom, checking to ensure they don't burn. Flip and fry until golden brown on the other side. Remove to a large paper towel–lined platter. Fry the remaining cutlets. Transfer the cutlets to a baking sheet and keep warm in a 200°F oven.

9. Carefully remove the shortening from the skillet and replace it with the bacon fat. Heat the bacon fat over medium heat and sauté the cremini, button and shiitake mushrooms for 8 minutes. Add the shallots and thyme and continue sautéing for 3 minutes.

10. Add the flour to the skillet and cook, stirring constantly, for 2 minutes. Stir in the Madeira.

11. Slowly pour in the stock (if you go too fast, it will clump), stirring constantly and scraping up the brown bits on the bottom of the skillet. Cook until the sauce thickens. Add the half-and-half and butter. Bring to a boil, stirring constantly, and then reduce the heat and simmer while you plate the chicken.

12. Put a breast and a thigh on each of 4 plates and ladle the gravy over the chicken. Crumble the crispy prosciutto on top and serve at once.

½ cup half-and-half (or substitute heavy cream for a slightly richer flavor)

3 tablespoons unsalted butter

FOR THE kiddos

Kids love to pound the chicken for this recipe and the rich sauce adds to their enjoyment of the dish. But the dish really grabs their attention when it's plated to create a forest scene!

SERVES 2

1 tablespoon unsalted butter

6 cremini mushrooms, with stems attached

1 chicken breast

1 Melt the butter in a medium saucepan over medium heat. Sauté the mushrooms until they are brown and tender but still hold their shape.

2 Pound the chicken breast to form a cutlet as in the adult recipe, and then cut out 4 forest-themed shapes, such as leaves or, better yet, bears. Bread the chicken and fry it as in the adult version.

3 Make the gravy according to the instructions in the adult recipe. Spoon some gravy on a plate so that it forms an S shape. Stand three mushrooms up along this gravy "path" and then prop one piece of chicken up against a mushroom "tree." Lay another piece of chicken on the plate. Repeat with the second plate and serve.

EASY LEMON CURRY CHICKEN
in Spicy Cream Sauce

You might be a little surprised, as I sure was, that kids take to this dish with gusto. Despite the name, both the chicken and the sauce are fairly mild, with just a hint of curry. I came up with this recipe for myself, because I wanted to spruce up some boring chicken breasts. They had a lovely yellow glaze, which caught Liam's and Stella's attention, and they asked me if they could have a taste. The monsters wolfed them down! The curry gives the dish an exotic flavor that is just pleasantly spicy but not overwhelming by any means. It's a great weeknight dish because it is simple and quick to whip up. You don't have to knock yourself out in the kitchen to create a knockout meal.

SERVES 4

1. Preheat the oven to 400°F.

2. In a small bowl, mix together the curry powder, cumin, salt and pepper. Sprinkle half the seasoning across a large platter. Set the chicken on the seasoning and then sprinkle the remaining seasoning on top. Pat the chicken to make the seasoning stick.

3. Heat the olive oil in a large nonstick skillet over medium-high heat. Sear each chicken breast on both sides until golden brown, about 8 minutes.

4. Transfer the chicken to a baking sheet and bake for 8 to 12 minutes, or until the internal temperature measures 165°F. Remove the chicken to a clean plate and loosely tent with foil to keep it warm while you prepare the sauce.

5. Add the lemon juice to the skillet in which the chicken was seared and cook over medium heat, scraping up any bits left from the chicken. Add 1 tablespoon of the butter, the curry powder, cumin, chili powder and coriander, and stir until the butter has melted.

6. Slowly whisk in the heavy cream. Bring the sauce to a boil, whisking continuously. Add the remaining 2 tablespoons butter and whisk until it melts. Season the sauce with salt and pepper.

7. Arrange the chicken on 4 individual plates and top with just enough sauce to cover. Serve at once.

Chicken

- 1 teaspoon curry powder
- 1 teaspoon ground cumin
- 1 teaspoon salt
- 2 teaspoons freshly cracked black pepper
- 4 boneless, skinless chicken breasts
- 2 tablespoons olive oil

Sauce

- ¼ cup lemon juice
- 1 tablespoon unsalted butter, plus 2 tablespoons
- 1 teaspoon curry powder
- ½ teaspoon ground cumin
- ¼ teaspoon chili powder
- ¼ teaspoon ground coriander
- ½ cup heavy cream
- Salt and freshly ground black pepper, to taste

FOR THE kiddos

Prepare the chicken as in the adult recipe, but put the tiniest amount of sauce on the chicken. Remember, we're trying to create young curry fans here. Garnish the chicken with a sprinkle of coarsely chopped parsley to add a little color and a few slices of steamed carrots. I also cut chicken into small morsels anytime I serve it to kids, because they like it best when it's bite-size and ready to eat.

POULET AU POIVRE

Bring a bit of Paris to your dinner table with this incredibly simple, rich and delicious twist on the French classic steak au poivre. I've kept my version simple, with a lush brandy-and-butter base that is true to the decadent original, and a healthy dose of the spice. The freshly cracked pepper is key to the savory bite in this dish. Loosen your pepper mill before grinding to crack the peppercorns. If you don't have a pepper mill, you can still get that sharp essence by cracking peppercorns by hand. Spread the peppercorns out on a cutting board covered with a sheet of parchment paper, run your hands lightly over them to spread them out, and place another sheet of parchment paper on top. Then use a heavy saucepan to coarsely grind the peppercorns, and, voilá, you've made the key ingredient old-school style!

SERVES 4

1. Preheat the oven to 400°F.

2. Season the chicken with 1½ tablespoons of the pepper and the salt.

3. Heat the oil in a large, heavy ovenproof skillet over medium heat. Cook the chicken, skin side down, until golden brown on the bottom, and then flip and brown the other side. Transfer the skillet to the oven and bake the chicken for 8 to 10 minutes, or until its internal temperature measures 165°F. Transfer the chicken to a large plate and loosely tent with foil.

4. Drain all but 1 tablespoon of the fat from the skillet you used for the chicken. Add the shallots and garlic, and sauté over medium heat until golden, about 3 minutes. Add the thyme and bay leaf. Add the brandy to deglaze the skillet, scraping up any bits stuck to the bottom. Cook until the liquid is reduced by half.

5. Add the cream, whisking continually, and bring it slowly to a boil. Add the butter one pat at a time, allow the sauce to absorb each pat completely before adding the next. Add the remaining ½ tablespoon pepper and the lemon juice. Taste and add salt, if desired. Remove the bay leaf and discard.

6. Cut each chicken breast into 5 even pieces, slicing diagonally toward the drumette. Arrange the sliced chicken breasts on 4 plates, top with the sauce, garnish with the parsley and serve.

4 boneless chicken breasts with drumettes attached (skin on)

1½ tablespoons freshly cracked black pepper, plus ½ tablespoon for the sauce

1 tablespoon salt, plus more for the sauce

1 tablespoon grapeseed or canola oil

1 shallot, peeled and finely diced

1 clove garlic, peeled and minced

1 tablespoon fresh thyme

1 bay leaf

½ cup brandy

¾ cup heavy cream

3 tablespoons unsalted butter, cut into 6 pats

Juice of ½ lemon

1 tablespoon chopped fresh parsley, for garnish

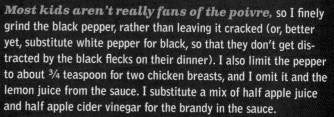
Most kids aren't really fans of the poivre, so I finely grind the black pepper, rather than leaving it cracked (or, better yet, substitute white pepper for black, so that they don't get distracted by the black flecks on their dinner). I also limit the pepper to about ¾ teaspoon for two chicken breasts, and I omit it and the lemon juice from the sauce. I substitute a mix of half apple juice and half apple cider vinegar for the brandy in the sauce.

Chicken pyramids tend to get the kids' attention. To make a chicken pyramid, cut the drumette from the cooked chicken breast and slice the breast lengthwise in an X pattern, to form four triangle-shaped pieces. Use the sauce as mortar for the chicken power towers. Place a pool of sauce on the plate and prop the triangles up side by side to form a pyramid (each triangle represents 1 side). Use sauce to "cement" the triangles together. Pool a little sauce to the side and stand the drumette up cut side down. Garnish with just a touch of parsley!

TURKEY PAN PIE

When I was a kid, I helped my dad build some horse stalls for a local farmer who did rodeo barrel racing. I was allowed to ride his horses if I cleaned the stalls out. For a thirteen-year-old, that was a pretty sweet deal. Plus, the farmer's wife sometimes made chicken potpie from scratch, and you could smell it cooking from a mile away. This is my interpretation of the tried-and-true potpie, the kind of true comfort food that makes for magical family meal memories. The secret is I cover the filling with plain and simple biscuits made with good old-fashioned buttermilk. Don't be afraid to get the kids involved in making the biscuits; they love dough, and the process is easy enough for even small children to handle. If you're a little tight on time, you can always use store-bought ready-to-bake biscuits and they'll still be really good. I especially like that this dish is served family style, all from one pan, but individual mini-casseroles or ramekins work, too.

SERVES 4

1. Preheat the oven to 425°F.

2. In a large bowl, whisk together the flour for the biscuits, along with the salt and pepper. Mix the butter into the flour mixture, squeezing it between your thumbs and fingers until you achieve a bread-crumb consistency. Do this fairly quickly so that the butter doesn't melt, which will create flat biscuits. If the butter gets too warm, place it back in the refrigerator or zap it in the freezer for a couple of minutes.

3. Create a well in the middle of the flour-butter mixture and pour in the buttermilk. Use a wooden spoon to stir until the batter starts to pull away from the sides of the bowl.

4. Flour a cutting board or other rolling surface, and roll the biscuit dough out to about ½ inch thick. Cut out biscuits with a 2-inch round cookie cutter (use a fun-shaped cutter for the kids). Reroll scraps and cut out more biscuits. Refrigerate the biscuits on a plate covered with plastic wrap.

5. In a small saucepan over high heat, combine 1 cup of the chicken stock, the potatoes, carrots and the ½ teaspoon salt.

6. Bring to a boil, then reduce to a simmer and cook until the vegetables are fork tender, 15 to 20 minutes. Drain the broth and reserve.

Buttermilk Biscuits

- **2** cups self-rising flour, plus extra for rolling out the dough
- **¼** teaspoon salt
- **¼** teaspoon black pepper
- **4** tablespoons cold unsalted butter, cut into small pats
- **¾** cup cold buttermilk

Filling

- **1** cup chicken stock, plus 2 cups
- **1** cup finely diced red potatoes
- **½** cup peeled and finely diced carrots
- **½** teaspoon salt
- **2** tablespoons unsalted butter
- **1** yellow onion, peeled and diced
- **½** cup finely diced celery
- **¼** teaspoon dry mustard
- **¼** teaspoon cayenne pepper
-     Salt and freshly ground black pepper, to taste
- **½** cup all-purpose flour
- **1** cup heavy cream
- **1** tablespoon fresh thyme leaves
- **½** cup frozen peas
- **2** cups cubed cooked turkey breast
- **1** large egg
- **3** tablespoons whole milk

continued on next page ›››

FOR THE kiddos

Kids will gobble this up and ask for more before you know it. Cut down on the cayenne pepper—or omit it entirely—for the youngsters. You can make it a little more fun for them by having them help out with the biscuits. They can cut out the biscuits with a turkey-shaped cutter (or any shape they want). You can also make it a little more personal by cooking the dish in mini pie tins or ramekins, so that every child has his or her own. You can even personalize their pies with alphabet cutters: let the kiddos cut out their own initials to top their dinner! Be sure to let the pies cool before serving.

7. In a large skillet, melt the butter over medium heat. Sauté the onions and celery until tender, about 6 minutes. Add the mustard, cayenne pepper, salt and pepper.

8. Sprinkle with the flour and cook, stirring constantly, until golden. Slowly whisk in the remaining and reserved chicken stock, and bring to a boil. Whisk in the heavy cream, and add thyme, peas and turkey. Stir to combine.

9. Pour into a 2½-quart oven-safe shallow baking dish. The turkey mixture should be nearly boiling when poured into the pan, which will help to ensure the biscuits cook evenly bottom to top.

10. Top with the biscuits. Do not crowd them. Make an egg wash by whisking the egg and milk together in a small bowl. Brush the biscuits with the egg wash. Season lightly with salt and pepper. Bake 15 to 20 minutes, or until golden brown. Let cool for 5 minutes and serve family style.

POACHED CHICKEN
in Tarragon White Wine Sauce

Sometimes you need to pull out all the stops and make something special for date night. This dish is a showcase of elegant, delicate flavors, but you need to taste it constantly as you make it, because it requires focus to make it correctly. It calls for some loving and careful attention, just like the person across the table from you. I like to pair this with a nice herb salad and a clean sauvignon blanc, to keep things light.

SERVES 2

1. Season the chicken breasts with salt and pepper.

2. Heat the olive oil in a medium pot over high heat. Sauté the mushrooms for 1 minute. Add the leeks, carrots and shallots and sauté for 3 minutes.

3. Add the wine, mustard, bay leaf and sprig of tarragon. Bring to a low boil and add the chicken breasts. Reduce the heat and simmer, covered, for 15 to 20 minutes, flipping the chicken a couple of times.

4. Transfer the chicken breasts to a plate and tent loosely with foil. Increase the heat to medium-high and cook the sauce until it starts to thicken. Then whisk in the butter, the remaining 2 teaspoons tarragon, the parsley and dill. Taste and adjust the seasoning.

5. Serve each chicken breast with a generous amount of sauce, 1 tablespoon of the crème fraîche and a dash of lemon zest. Garnish with 2 sprigs of dill and lemon wheels.

2 boneless, skinless chicken breasts, pounded ¼ inch thick

Salt and freshly ground black pepper, to taste

2 tablespoons olive oil

2 cups coarsely chopped porcini mushrooms

½ cup julienned leeks (white part only)

1 carrot, peeled and julienned

2 tablespoons minced shallots

1 cup dry white wine

1 tablespoon Dijon mustard

1 bay leaf

1 sprig fresh tarragon, plus 2 teaspoons chopped

3 tablespoons unsalted butter

2 tablespoons minced fresh parsley

2 teaspoons minced fresh dill, plus 4 sprigs, for garnish

2 tablespoons crème fraîche

Zest of ½ lemon

½ lemon, cut into ¼-inch slices, for wheel garnish

FOR THE kiddos

I whip them up something a little sweeter and less delicate. Poach two boneless, skinless chicken breasts in 1 cup white grape juice. Remove the chicken and keep warm. Make the sauce simple and delicious, with just button mushrooms, leeks, carrots and 2 tablespoons minced parsley. Reduce the sauce and finish it with butter and herbs. Then shred the chicken breasts, toss in the sauce and serve on mini slider buns (or cut out shapes from any bread and serve open-faced). Nothing like mini sandwiches to put smiles on the little ones' faces.

My Kids' Favorite
BLACK-AND-WHITE CHICKEN FINGERS

Chicken fingers were practically invented for a houseful of kids—which is why I turn to them on a regular basis. But the Gourmet Dad can't just make plain old chicken fingers. I add some visual interest and engaging but kid-friendly flavors. Adding black and white sesame seeds really grabs children's interest without adding any work to one of the simplest recipes you'll find. A word of advice from experience—make sure you buy true chicken tenders, which are incredibly tender flaps of meat from under the chicken breast. Many "tenders" are just sliced-up breast meat.

¾ cup honey, heated

1 cup black and white sesame seeds

¼ teaspoon salt

¼ teaspoon black pepper

1 pound chicken tenders

SERVES 4

1. Preheat the oven to 425°F. Line a baking sheet with parchment paper and set aside.

2. Pour the honey into a small shallow dish. Combine the sesame seeds, salt and pepper in a second small shallow dish.

3. Coat the chicken tenders, working with 1 tender at a time. Dip half of a chicken tender in the honey and then dredge it in the sesame-seed mixture. Transfer the chicken tender to the prepared baking sheet. Coat the rest of the chicken tenders the same way.

4. Bake the tenders until they are golden and cooked through, about 20 minutes.

FRIED CHICKEN AND JALAPEÑO WAFFLES
with Maple, Honey and Chili Drizzle

Chicken and waffles has long been a classic anytime dish down South. I took the basic fried chicken and plain waffles and cranked the flavors up to eleven. The blank slate of slightly sweet waffles is just about the perfect canvas for a bit of heat courtesy of jalapeños, and combining honey and chili pepper in a syrup substitute makes this one super-interesting dish.

SERVES 4

1. In a small saucepan, combine the maple syrup, ⅓ cup water, honey, crushed red pepper flakes and Tabasco sauce. Bring to a boil over medium heat, and then reduce the heat and simmer for 3 minutes. Remove from the heat and set aside.

2. Preheat the oven to 400°F.

3. Set the chicken parts on a plate, and cover. Set aside and allow to come to room temperature.

4. Place the jalapeños in a small baking dish, and bake for 20 minutes. After baking, you'll need to char the jalapeños. If you have a gas range, turn a burner to a low flame. Place the jalapeños right on the burner and rotate until just blackened. If you have an electric range, skewer the jalapeños and roast like you are roasting a marshmallow. Set them aside to cool. Reduce the oven temperature to 250°F.

5. In a large bowl, mix together the flour, baking powder, sugar and salt. In a medium bowl, whisk the eggs and then add the milk, butter and vanilla extract until well combined. Add the wet ingredients into the dry mixture, and mix well with a fork. Pour half the waffle batter into a medium bowl and designate this the kids' bowl. The large bowl will be the grown-ups' bowl. Finely dice the reserved jalapeños, add them to the grown-up batter and mix well.

6. Prepare the waffles. Brush both sides of a waffle iron with vegetable oil and preheat. (If you don't own a waffle iron, you can make thin pancakes with the batter instead.) Follow the manufacturer's instructions for making waffles. (Waffle irons come in many shapes and sizes, and they call for varying amounts of batter.)

7. Make the kids' waffles first and the adults' second, because you don't want to get any jalapeño flavor on the kids' waffles. When you

continued on next page >>>

Maple, Honey and Chili Drizzle

- ½ cup pure maple syrup
- ¼ cup honey
- 1 teaspoon crushed red pepper flakes, or to taste
- ½ teaspoon Tabasco sauce, or to taste

Waffles

- 2 jalapeño peppers
- 2 cups all-purpose flour
- 4 teaspoons baking powder
- 2 teaspoons granulated sugar
- ½ teaspoon salt
- 2 large eggs
- 1½ cups warm milk
- 1 cup unsalted butter, melted
- 1 teaspoon pure vanilla extract
- Vegetable oil, for cooking the waffles

Chicken

- 4 chicken drumsticks (skin on, bone in)
- 4 chicken thighs (skin on, bone in)
- 2 cups canola oil (or more, depending on the size of your pan or fryer)
- 2 cups cornflakes
- 1 cup all-purpose flour, plus 1 cup
- 2 large eggs
- 2 tablespoons whole milk
- Salt and freshly ground black pepper, to taste
- 3 scallions, root ends removed and thinly sliced, for garnish

finish a batch of waffles, place them on a baking sheet, and pop them in a 250°F oven to keep them warm while you make the rest.

8. Prepare the chicken. If you're using a deep fryer, turn it on now and heat the oil to 340°F. In a food processor, pulse the cornflakes to a chunky bread-crumb consistency. Pour the cornflakes into a large bowl and mix in 1 cup of the flour. In a small bowl, whisk together the eggs and milk. In a third bowl, mix the remaining 1 cup flour with the salt and pepper.

9. Bread the chicken drumsticks and thighs by rolling a piece of chicken in the flour until completely covered and tapping off any excess. Dip the chicken in the egg-milk mixture, coating well, and then roll it in the cornflakes. Really press down on the chicken to drive that crispy coating into the skin and help it stick. Place the breaded chicken on a large plate and coat the rest of the chicken.

10. If you are not using a deep fryer, heat 1 inch of oil in a deep-sided frying pan over medium-high heat. Do not fill the frying pan more than halfway. Heat the oil in the deep fryer or frying pan to 340°F. (I prefer this temperature since I can leave the chicken in the fryer for a little while longer to make it really crispy without burning the outside coating.)

11. Fry 2 pieces of chicken in the frying pan for 5 to 8 minutes per side, or until golden brown and crispy. (Or use your deep fryer.) Remove the chicken to a paper towel–lined plate. Check the internal temperature of the chicken with a thermometer. (The USDA recommends an internal temperature of 165°F for chicken to be safe to eat.)

12. For adults, put 2 jalapeño waffles on each plate and stack 2 pieces of chicken on top. Spoon some of the Maple, Honey and Chili Drizzle over the top, and garnish with the scallions. For kids, put 1 waffle on a plate and top with 1 piece of chicken. Serve with maple syrup in a ramekin or a small cup on the side so that the kids have the option to dip or pour the syrup over their chicken and waffles.

ICKY, STICKY CHICKEN

Is it one of those nights when you just need a guaranteed "no battle at dinnertime, smiles around the table, easy to make" kid pleaser? Look no further. Easy and quick to make, this chicken dish includes only simple spices and sweetness that kids universally love. Plus, it's just as great as a snack for the grown-ups. If you're serving it as a quick bite for the adults, add some crushed red pepper flakes to the honey to give it a little heat. Marinate some thinly sliced red cabbage in a little rice wine, and roll the chicken and cabbage up in butter lettuce. Finish with some lime juice and zest, and watch your guests swarm. I recommend buying one normal-size boneless, skinless chicken breast per person. Family-size, jumbo breasts are tricky to cook evenly, so smaller is better.

4 boneless, skinless chicken breasts

¼ cup cornstarch

¼ cup self-rising flour

Salt and freshly ground white pepper, to taste

1 cup vegetable oil (or more, depending on the size of your pan or fryer)

½ cup honey

SERVES 4

1. Rinse the chicken breasts and pat them dry. Cut them crosswise into long strips about ¼ inch wide, and then cut the strips in half.

2. In a small mixing bowl, combine the cornstarch, flour, and a pinch of salt and white pepper.

3. In a large frying pan over high heat, heat the oil.

4. Dredge the chicken in the flour mix. Knock off the excess flour, and then slide the chicken into the pan, in 2 batches if necessary (to prevent crowding) until golden brown, about 5 minutes per side.

5. Arrange the chicken on a plate, sprinkle lightly with salt, if desired, and then drizzle with honey, rotating each piece to coat. Serve with plain rice, fries or potato chips, and with thinly sliced carrots, and watch it disappear.

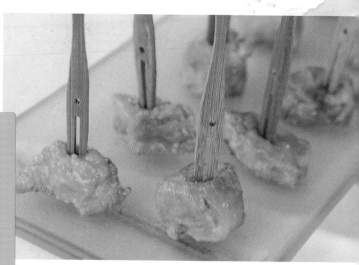

Dean's Food 411

I use white pepper to bring out the flavor of the chicken. This works well with kids, since they don't like seeing little black pepper specks. If you don't have white pepper, just omit it from the recipe. White pepper is a great pantry staple because you can use it for things like mashed potatoes and sauces, where black pepper specks would be questioned.

Chapter four

HIDES

It might have been a Canadian thing, or maybe just a "broke and stretching the grocery budget" thing, but every year my mom would place a gigantic "freezer order" with a big meat and canned goods company. My friends and I would wait with bated breath for a huge refrigerated truck to rumble down our street. They'd be delivering essentially a whole year's supply of meat and canned foods, and my friends and I couldn't wait to help unload the truck with the delivery guys. We felt pretty tough. A couple of us would roll a dolly of food into the house and then take turns riding on it on the way back to the truck.

But I could have done without the unloading. It was a sad preview—a warning, really—of the culinary fate that awaited me in the months to come. A big package labeled "ground chuck" meant gamey, dry hamburgers with big, nearly indigestible pieces of onion and green pepper sticking out. The one with "chuck roast" printed on it meant stringy, chewy Sunday dinners and Mom's gelatinous "Chunky" beef stew. Fifteen-pound waxed bolognas meant dreary school lunches and ridicule for a year. And there was my nemesis: liver. Don't even get me started. Liver was pure, sheer torture. To this day I cannot eat liver.

On my way to becoming a dad—and eventually the Gourmet Dad—I vowed to give my kids a better experience with all kinds of meat. I didn't want them thinking that anything had to be forced down or suffered through. It can be a bit of a challenge sometimes, because kids just aren't naturally big meat lovers. The trick is to offer a diversity of different proteins in recipes with interesting but not overwhelming flavors, and to create intrigue with how you plate the food. That can go a long way toward full stomachs and empty plates.

With that in mind, I've filled this chapter with a good mix of different meats and different cooking styles. I've included some tried-and-true old family dinner table classics (with a few new twists), like pork chops and applesauce, but I have also thrown in dishes full of ways to prepare "lesser" cuts of meat and turned them into rave reviews around the table. Cooking for a family inevitably means watching the old wallet (the main reason my mom went with the freezer order every year), so I try to use beef, pork and lamb cuts that are inexpensive but super-tasty done the Gourmet Dad way. I've also thrown in some nicer cuts, like sirloins and fillets, for when you want to splurge. With these recipes in your arsenal, your little ones should prepare to "meat" their match! If all else fails, you can tell my freezer-order story as your own and guilt them into eating.

MINER'S STEAK—TWO WAYS

Sometimes there's nothing better than a well-cooked steak. And as much as I love to fire up the grill, panfrying is an incredible way to prepare a cut of meat. Nothing keeps a steak super juicy all the way through the panfrying process like butter. Butter adds a rich sweetness that complements the natural flavor of the meat. Here's another secret grill masters and chefs know, but many people never catch on to: the only seasonings you need for a nice steak are salt and pepper. Period. But a great steak starts with the meat you buy, so I recommend buying USDA Choice. It costs a little more than USDA Select, but it's worth it.

SERVES 4

4 steaks, strip loin (New York strip) or rib eye, 1 to 1½ inches thick

Salt and freshly cracked black pepper, to season

2 tablespoons unsalted butter

3 to 4 sprigs fresh thyme

1. Preheat the oven to 300°F. Pat the steaks dry and season all over with the salt and pepper. Let them come to room temperature.

2. Preheat a large cast-iron frying pan over high heat. Add the butter and thyme. Let the butter bubble, but be careful that it doesn't burn.

3. Test if the frying pan is hot enough by dipping a corner of one of the steaks into the butter, which should sizzle and pop. Lay the steaks in the pan and do not flip. (If necessary, fry the steaks in two groups.) Tilt the pan, collect the butter in a tablespoon and spoon it over the steaks. Gently keep the pan and butter moving so that the butter doesn't burn.

4. Cook the steaks for 2 to 3 minutes per side, or until well browned. Use tongs to gently pull up one corner of each steak. If they come up cleanly, they're ready to flip. After both sides are cooked, salt each steak and pop the pan into the oven for 3 to 5 minutes. Remove the steaks from the pan and let them rest for at least 5 minutes. Discard the thyme.

5. Serve the steaks with a side of your choice. The potatoes and asparagus in the kids' version is pretty great, or try the Rainbow Chard with Bacon and Capers on page 164.

Dean's Food 411

Letting a steak or any cut of meat rest after cooking allows the juices to settle back into the meat, and the meat to continue cooking for a short period. If you cut into it or carve it too soon, the meat will release all the juices, and you end up with dry meat and a puddle of flavorful juices on your plate or cutting board.

FOR THE **kiddos**

The kids' version is actually where the name of this dish comes from, because I make my kids dig for treasure and eat their meal along the way, and I use bite-size everything. A little knife work goes a long way toward getting the kiddies to clean their plates.

SERVES 2 TO 4

4 russet potatoes, peeled and quartered

Two 8-ounce rib eye, sirloin or flank steaks (or substitute hamburgers)

Salt and freshly ground white pepper, to taste

One 14.5-ounce can whole corn (or substitute 2 cups fresh corn kernels cut off the cob)

½ cup whole milk

¼ cup unsalted butter

½ teaspoon olive oil

8 cooked broccoli spears

8 cooked asparagus tips (trimmed to 3 inches in length)

1 Fill a large pot halfway with salted water. Add the potatoes and bring to a boil over high heat. Reduce the heat to medium and cook the potatoes until they are fork-tender, about 20 minutes. Drain and return to the pot. Set the pot on the burner and turn off the heat.

2 While the potatoes are cooking, pat the steaks dry and season with salt and pepper on both sides. Set aside and allow the steaks to come to room temperature.

3 Warm the corn in a small pot over low heat. If using fresh corn, boil for 5 minutes and then drain.

4 Preheat the oven to 350°F.

5 Bring the milk and butter to a boil in a small pot over medium-high heat and then remove from the heat. Mash the potatoes in a large bowl until they have a smooth, consistent texture. Do not overwork, or they will become sticky and pasty. Fold in the milk-butter mixture and season with salt and pepper. Cover the potatoes and keep them warm.

6 Heat the olive oil in a large frying pan over high heat, add the steaks and sear them, about 3 minutes per side. Finish the steaks in the oven, cooking them for about 5 minutes, or until they are medium. (When you see juices rise to the top of your steak, it's medium.) Adjust the cooking time if your kids like a different degree of doneness. Remove the steaks to a cutting board, let them rest for at least 5 minutes and then cut into bite-size pieces.

7 To serve, put a mound of potatoes just off center on each of the plates. Hollow out the middle of each mound with a teaspoon, creating a little igloo. Fill the hollow with the corn. Pile the pieces of steak up in front of the corn until you can't see it. Make a forest of trees on top of the potatoes with the broccoli and asparagus. Tell the kids to search for gold (the corn) in the mine-shaft entrance. They can use either a spoon or their fingers. They have to eat the fallen boulders (steak) to get to the gold.

PORK CHOPSCHS AND APPLE SAUSCH

This is a family favorite that kids will devour. My mom used to panfry her pork chops to death; we could have used them as bulletproof vests. I brine my pork chops to ensure that they never, ever dry out, and pair them with applesauce. In case you're wondering, this one is named for how Liam and, of course, Peter Brady used to pronounce it.

SERVES 4

1. Prepare the brine. In a large bowl, mix together ¾ cup boiling water, salt, sugar and pepper. Stir to dissolve the sugar. Add 12 cups cold water. Submerge the chops in the brine, cover and refrigerate for at least 2 hours, but preferably overnight (use a brining bag if the pot won't fit in the refrigerator).

2. Remove the chops from the brine and pat dry with paper towels. Heat a grill pan, outdoor grill or frying pan over medium-high heat. Add the vegetable oil to the frying pan, or use it to brush the grill pan or grill grates. Panfry or grill the chops for 4 to 6 minutes per side, or until they reach the desired doneness. The internal temperature should be between 145°F (medium) and 160°F (well done). Take the chops off the heat 10 degrees shy of your intended temperature. (They will continue to cook while they are resting.)

3. Prepare the fruit. Make two equal piles of apples and pears. Add the fennel to one pile. This will be the grown-up pile. Melt 2 tablespoons of butter in each of two medium frying pans over medium heat. Put the grown-up pile of apples, pears and fennel in one pan, and the kids' pile in the other.

4. Add the vinegar, brown sugar, cinnamon and salt to the adults' pan. Add the agave nectar to the kids' pan. Cook, stirring occasionally, until the fruit has softened slightly, about 5 minutes for the kids' pan and 8 minutes for the adults'.

5. When serving adults, arrange 1 pork chop on each of 4 plates and cover with the apple-pear-fennel medley.

Brine

¼ cup coarse kosher salt

¼ cup granulated sugar

1 tablespoon freshly ground black pepper

Chops

4 center-cut (loin or rib) pork chops, bone in and 1 to 1¼ inches thick

2 tablespoons vegetable oil

Fruit

4 sweet apples, peeled, cored and cut into ⅛-inch slices

2 pears, peeled, cored and cut into ⅛-inch slices

1 fennel bulb, stem trimmed and cut into ⅛-inch slices

4 tablespoons unsalted butter

2 tablespoons apple cider vinegar

1 tablespoon light brown sugar

Pinch of ground cinnamon

Pinch of salt

3 tablespoons agave nectar

Dean's Food 411

Kids love to dip—and interact with—their food. Anytime you can put a sauce or a dip in a separate serving dish, do it. Believe me, this will make your life a whole lot easier.

FOR THE **kiddos**

I set up the prep for this dish to get the meal on the table ASAP. So if you've made the adult version, just run the apples and pears through a food processor or blender until smooth for the kids. Strain with a fine strainer to remove the excess liquid. Serve the apple-pear sauce in small ramekins or cups, and cut the pork chops into bite-size chunks. Dinner is ready!

Tricolor
SHEPHERD'S PIE

The Brits traditionally use mutton in this filling working-man's dinner, which is where the name comes from. It works just as well with ground beef or even ground turkey, but I'm a lamb man. And instead of the traditional plain mashed potatoes, I've flavored the potatoes and created three kinds of potato toppings, so the dish has something for everyone.

SERVES 6

1. Peel all the potatoes and cut them into 1-inch cubes, keeping them separated. Put the sweet potatoes in one medium pot, and the other potatoes in a second medium pot. Cover all the potatoes with cold water. Bring both pots to a boil over medium heat, season with salt, and then reduce the heat and simmer until the potatoes are tender but not falling apart, about 15 minutes. Drain the potatoes and return them to their respective pots.

2. In a separate pot over medium-high heat, combine the milk and butter, and stir until the butter is melted. Divide the mixture between the two pots of potatoes.

3. Season both pots with salt and pepper, remove from the heat and mash the potatoes with a masher. (You can also use a hand mixer or immersion blender.) Taste and add more salt and pepper, if desired.

4. Mix the honey and the chipotle pepper into the sweet potatoes.

5. Combine the peas, mint and heavy cream in a blender and puree on high until smooth. (You may need to add extra cream to puree.) Combine half of the russet potato mix in a separate pot with the pea puree, and stir until fully incorporated. Season with salt, pepper and the lemon zest.

6. Preheat the oven to 400°F.

7. Heat the oil in a large sauté pan over medium-high heat, and sauté the onions, fennel, carrots and parsnips until tender, about 7 minutes. Stir in the garlic. Add the lamb and cook until browned, about 10 minutes. Spoon out any excess fat as the lamb cooks and break up any clumps of meat with a fork or potato masher.

8. Add the stock, tomato paste and oregano. Bring the mixture to a boil, and then reduce the heat to medium and cook for a few

continued on next page >>>

Potato Toppings

1 large Yukon Gold potato, peeled and cut into 1-inch cubes

1 medium russet potato, peeled and cut into 1-inch cubes

1 large sweet potato, peeled and cut into 1-inch cubes

Salt and freshly ground black pepper, to taste

1/2 cup whole milk

1 stick unsalted butter, sliced into pats

1 teaspoon honey

1/2 teaspoon chopped chipotle pepper in adobo sauce

1 cup frozen peas, thawed

1/2 cup chopped fresh mint

2 to 4 tablespoons heavy cream

Zest of 1 lemon

Pie Filling

1 tablespoon canola oil

1 yellow onion, peeled and chopped

1 fennel bulb, stem trimmed and chopped

1 carrot, peeled and chopped

1 parsnip, peeled and chopped

1 clove garlic, peeled and minced

1 pound lean ground lamb

1 cup beef stock

1 tablespoon tomato paste

1 tablespoon chopped fresh oregano

CONTINUED...

minutes, or until the filling thickens slightly (it will still be some-what liquid). Fold in the corn, peas and chives.

9. Pour the filling into a 9 x 13-inch baking dish and then turn the baking dish so that the long side faces you. Spread the mashed sweet potatoes across the top third of the filling, making a stripe. Next, spread the plain mashed russet potatoes across the middle, making a center stripe. Finally, spread the mashed potatoes with peas across the bottom third of the filling. (You can spread the three potato toppings in any order you wish.) Top the plain mashed russet potatoes with a sprinkling of Parmesan, if desired.

10. Bake the shepherd's pie for 25 to 30 minutes, or until the top starts to brown. Let cool for 5 minutes before serving.

½ cup fresh corn kernels (or substitute frozen off-season)

½ cup fresh peas (or substitute frozen off-season)

1 tablespoon minced fresh chives

¼ cup grated Parmesan cheese (optional)

FOR THE kiddos

Mash it up! Kids love going to town on mashed potatoes, so hand them a masher and let them get to work. I usually make plain mashed potatoes for the kids' version, and I bake and serve the shepherd's pie in individual ramekins or small casserole dishes. Get your little ones even more involved by spooning the mashed potatoes into a pastry bag and letting them pipe the potatoes over the filling, making any design they like. Sprinkle a little Parmesan cheese over the top of the finished product and bake it like you would the adult version. Cool for 5 to 10 minutes before serving.

Tori's Favorite
BEEF BOURGUIGNON

This is Tori's favorite dish, and I think I know why. The original started out as a French peasant stew and, thanks largely to Julia Child, came to represent really upscale haute cuisine. My version captures the spirit of the original with a great mix of down-to-earth, complementary herbs and savory, robust flavors. It's not too heavy, just wonderfully delicious and satisfying in every possible way. So I guess Tori likes it because it reminds her of her husband. And I make it a lot, because when Mom's happy, everybody's happy.

SERVES 6

1. Preheat the oven to 300°F.

2. Place the beef on a baking sheet lined with paper towels. Season both sides with salt, pepper and 2 tablespoons chopped thyme. Let the meat sit at room temperature for at least 30 minutes.

3. Heat 1 tablespoon of the oil in a Dutch oven over high heat and sear the beef cubes on all sides, working in batches. Be careful not to overcrowd the Dutch oven. Reduce the heat to medium after the initial batch goes in. Remove the seared beef to a large bowl and set aside.

4. Next, sauté the pancetta in the Dutch oven until it starts to brown, about 3 minutes. Remove to a plate. Sauté the carrots for 1 minute, and then add the yellow onions and continue sautéing until the onions have browned, about 7 minutes. Add the garlic, stir and deglaze with the brandy. Cook until the liquid is reduced by half.

5. Stir in the tomato paste and then return the beef and pancetta and any accumulated juices to the Dutch oven. Pour in the wine and stock, adding enough stock to just cover the meat, and then bring to a boil. Reduce the heat, add the other 1 tablespoon chopped thyme, the parsley sprigs and the bay leaf and simmer, covered, until the beef is tender, about 2 to 2½ hours.

6. Meanwhile, heat the remaining 1 tablespoon olive oil in a large skillet over medium heat and sauté the pearl onions and mushrooms until tender and slightly browned. Set aside until the meat has finished cooking.

3 pounds chuck roast, any excess fat trimmed and cubed

2 teaspoons kosher salt

2 tablespoons freshly cracked black pepper

3½ tablespoons chopped thyme leaves

1 tablespoon olive oil, plus 1 tablespoon for sautéing the pearl onions

½ pound pancetta, cut into ¼-inch strips (lardons—substitute thick-cut bacon as necessary)

1 carrot, peeled and sliced

1 yellow onion, peeled and sliced

3 cloves garlic, peeled and smashed

½ cup brandy

1 tablespoon tomato paste

1 bottle red burgundy wine (or substitute any other hearty red wine)

2 to 3 cups beef stock

6 sprigs fresh parsley, plus ½ teaspoon minced, for garnish

1 bay leaf

24 pearl onions, skins removed

1 pound cremini mushrooms, quartered

2 tablespoons unsalted butter, at room temperature

2 tablespoons all-purpose flour

Juice of ½ lemon

continued on next page ›››

7. Once the beef is fork-tender, remove it from the Dutch oven and
   strain it over a large heatproof bowl using a mesh strainer. Return
   the broth to the Dutch oven and bring to a boil.

8. In a small bowl, combine the butter and flour, and mix well. Whisk
   vigorously into the broth. Bring the broth to a boil, and then reduce
   the heat and simmer until it has thickened. Stir in the lemon juice.

9. Return the meat to the Dutch oven, and stir in the reserved onions
   and mushrooms. Heat through and serve hot, garnished with the
   remaining ½ tablespoon thyme and the minced parsley.

 FOR THE **kiddos**

A stew like this can give kids pause because a full plate is just too "beefy" for them. I head off any complaints by baking up little single servings, making the dish manage-able for small eyes and appetites. Buy a store-bought pastry crust and cut it into 2½-inch squares. Line the wells of a muffin tin with the squares and then prick the bottoms slightly with a fork. Brush with a tablespoon of melted butter and bake at 375°F until golden brown, 12 to 15 minutes. Poke a hole in the top of the cups. Fill the flaky cups with a few spoonfuls of the stew, avoiding anything that turns your child off. Nice and uniform is the way to go here.

Tomato and Short Rib
NOODLE CASSEROLE

Me and short ribs are good friends. It's not just that they're inexpensive (though that's nice). The real reason is the delectable, tender meat. All you need to create an unforgettable dish like this one is some short ribs, an acidic base (the tomatoes here) and a little bit of time for braising. The liquid loosens the fibers of the meat, and it becomes fall-off-the-bone tender, not to mention having flavor for days. You can use any pasta here, but if my kids are any indication, you could pretty much serve it over shoelaces and they'd finish this meat right off.

SERVES 6

1. Preheat the oven to 300°F.

2. Drizzle the olive oil over the short ribs on all sides and season with the rosemary, salt and pepper. Let the meat come to room temperature before cooking.

3. Heat a Dutch oven over high heat until it smokes. Reduce the heat to medium-high and sear the short ribs in batches. Transfer the seared short ribs to a clean plate and set aside.

4. Add the quartered onion, quartered carrot and smashed garlic cloves to the Dutch oven and sauté for 5 minutes, scraping the bottom of the pot while they cook.

5. Return the short ribs to the Dutch oven and add 1 can of the tomatoes, pouring in only enough of the tomato juice to cover the meat by three-quarters. Add the bunch of basil, cover and cook in the oven for 2 hours, or until the meat is fork-tender.

6. Heat a 6-quart or larger stockpot filled with water over high heat. When the water comes to a boil, salt it heavily. Boil the pasta for three-quarters of the cooking time noted on the package. Be careful not to overcook it, because it will finish cooking in the oven later. Drain and spread the pasta on a baking sheet. Drizzle with olive oil and toss to coat. Set aside.

7. Once the ribs are tender, remove them from the oven and increase the temperature to 400°F. Discard the basil. Use a slotted spoon to remove the meat, and set aside. Mash the tomatoes and vegetables in the Dutch oven with a potato masher to make a sauce. Once the short ribs are cool enough to handle, shred them with a fork or your fingers.

1 tablespoon olive oil, plus more for drizzling on the pasta

2 pounds boneless beef short ribs

2 tablespoons chopped fresh rosemary

1 teaspoon salt

1 teaspoon freshly cracked black pepper

1 yellow onion, peeled and quartered, plus 1 peeled and diced

1 carrot, peeled and quartered, plus 1 peeled and diced

3 cloves garlic, peeled and smashed, plus 2 cloves peeled and minced

Two 28-ounce cans whole San Marzano tomatoes

1 bunch fresh basil, plus ½ cup slightly torn basil leaves

One 16-ounce box gemelli pasta

2 tablespoons unsalted butter

1 large zucchini, ends trimmed and diced

1 cup diced cremini mushrooms

½ teaspoon crushed red pepper flakes, or to taste

¼ cup finely grated Parmigiano-Reggiano cheese, plus ¼ cup for topping

2 tablespoons finely grated Romano cheese, plus 2 tablespoons for topping

8. Heat a large sauté pan over high heat. Add the butter and sauté the diced onions until tender and barely caramelized, about 3 minutes. Add the minced garlic, diced carrots, zucchini and mushrooms, and cook until tender and golden, about 5 minutes.

9. Use your fingers to break up the remaining can of tomatoes. Add the tomatoes, pulled short rib meat, red pepper flakes and cooked pasta to the sauté pan. Toss gently to coat with the sauce. (Note: The short ribs and pasta should be slightly wet because they will be baked. If they are too dry, add some of the reserved liquid from the tomatoes.)

10. Add ¼ cup Parmigiano-Reggiano and 2 tablespoons Romano. Spoon the mixture into an oiled 9 x 13-inch casserole dish and top with the remaining cheese. Bake for about 20 minutes, or until bubbly and golden. Finish under the broiler, if desired, to get a slightly crispy and golden crust.

FOR THE kiddos

I like to mix this up by making spaghetti cupcakes. You read it right: cupcakes. Out of spaghetti. Here's how you do it.

SERVES 2 TO 4

1 Preheat the oven to 400°F.

2 Cook half a box of spaghetti to al dente. Combine it with 1 to 2 cups (depending on the number of kids) of the adult short ribs with tomato sauce (don't mix the gemelli into the sauce in the adults' recipe until after removing short ribs and sauce for the kids) and ¾ cup grated Parmesan cheese. Toss and set aside.

3 Generously oil the wells of a muffin tin and twirl the spaghetti-beef mixture into each well, pressing down to ensure a cupcake shape. Top with ¼ cup grated Parmesan and bake until golden and slightly crispy, about 20 to 25 minutes. Serve hot and watch the smiles.

BEEF-AND-ONION LEMONGRASS KEBABS
on Jeweled Fragrant Rice

The "jeweled" rice in this dish is as pretty as it is delicious. I use basmati rice because it has an incredible aroma and flavor. It's also fluffier than other types of rice and is less prone to clumping. It's a little pricier than standard white rice, but for this dish, it's well worth the added cost. However, if you can't find basmati or just don't want to pony up the extra coin, substitute jasmine rice, long-grain rice or even Minute Rice. Just be aware that cooking times vary for the different rices, so read the instructions.

SERVES 4 TO 6

1. Soak 12 wooden skewers in water for at least 30 minutes to prevent them from burning on the grill.

2. Prepare the marinade for the beef. Break open the lemongrass stalk by hitting it with the back of a heavy chef's knife. Slice the stalk into 1-inch pieces. Place the lemongrass pieces, coconut oil, chili pepper, garlic, honey, cilantro, cumin seeds and coriander seeds in a blender and process on high until smooth.

3. Place the beef cubes in a shallow baking dish and season with salt and pepper, coat with the lemongrass puree and sprinkle with the lime zest. Massage the marinade into the meat, cover with plastic wrap and refrigerate for at least 30 minutes, but preferably 2 hours.

4. Meanwhile, make the rice. Heat 1 tablespoon oil in a small saucepot over medium-high heat, add the yellow onions and sauté until translucent. Add the curry powder and sauté for 30 seconds, or until the curry smell is strong.

5. Add the rice and stir to coat. Pour in the chicken stock and bring to a boil. Reduce the heat, cover, and simmer for 20 minutes. Remove the rice from the heat, add the butter and fluff the rice gently with a fork. Mix in the cashews, raisins, cilantro, cumin seeds, pomegranate seeds and salt. Set the rice aside and keep warm.

6. Assemble the kebabs. Remove the beef cubes from the marinade. Discard the marinade. Slide 1 tomato onto a skewer, followed by a beef cube, a red onion wedge and a zucchini round. Alternate the ingredients until all the kebabs are assembled. Brush all sides of the kebabs generously with the remaining 3 tablespoons oil.

Kebabs

- 1 stalk fresh lemongrass
- ¼ cup coconut oil, liquefied
- 1 Fresno chili pepper, seeded and chopped, or to taste
- 3 cloves garlic, peeled
- 2 teaspoons honey
- 2 teaspoons chopped fresh cilantro, plus 12 cilantro leaves for garnish
- 2 teaspoons cumin seeds, toasted and ground (or substitute ground cumin)
- 1 teaspoon coriander seeds, toasted and ground (or substitute ground coriander)
- 2 pounds boneless beef sirloin, cubed
- Salt and pepper, to taste
- Zest and juice of 2 limes, separated
- 12 baby Roma tomatoes (or substitute cherry tomatoes)
- 1 small red onion, peeled and cut into wedges through the core
- 1 zucchini, ends trimmed and cut into ½-inch rounds

"Jeweled" Rice

- 1 tablespoon vegetable oil, plus 3 tablespoons for the kebabs
- ¼ cup minced yellow onion
- 1 teaspoon yellow curry powder
- 1½ cups basmati rice (or substitute the rice of your choosing)
- 2 cups chicken stock
- 2 tablespoons unsalted butter, at room temperature

CONTINUED...

Grill over medium-high heat, rotating, for about 6 to 10 minutes (6 minutes for rare, 8 minutes for medium rare and 10 minutes for medium). Or put the kebabs under the broiler and broil for 5 to 8 minutes per side.

7. Squeeze the lime juice over the kebabs and sprinkle with a touch of salt and pepper, if desired, as they come off the grill. Serve over a mound of "jeweled" rice and garnish with cilantro leaves.

½ cup toasted cashews

¼ cup raisins (or substitute currants or dried cranberries)

¼ cup fresh cilantro

¼ teaspoon cumin seeds, toasted and ground (or substitute ground cumin)

3 tablespoons fresh or frozen pomegranate seeds (or substitute dried cranberries or currants)

Salt, to taste

DEAN'S STUFFED ITALIAN BURGERS

Having five kids means I'm not bored during the day, and when it comes time to get dinner on the table, I'm not going to cook a boring meal—especially when I fire up my grill. There's just no excuse for a boring burger. I grind up my own meat for an incredibly fresh flavor (you can also ask a butcher to do this for you), and I use three different Italian meats. Add in a bevy of Italian spices, and you wind up with an American grilling classic that speaks with a strong Italian accent. It's a totally different type of burger and anything but boring.

SERVES 4

1. Combine all the ingredients for the aioli in a blender or food processor and blend until nearly smooth. Transfer the aioli to a small bowl, cover and refrigerate.

2. Line a baking sheet with parchment paper. Spread the sirloin, salami, prosciutto and cappicola on the baking sheet and place in the freezer for 20 minutes, or until the outside of the sirloin is hard but the sirloin is not frozen through.

3. In a large mixing bowl, toss all the meats with the pepperoncini, garlic and red pepper flakes. In a stand mixer with a meat grinder attachment, grind the meats together on medium. (If you don't have a grinder, have a butcher grind the meats for you, and then simply mix in the pepperoncini, garlic and red pepper flakes. Mince the garlic first.) Shape the meat mixture into four equal patties. Brush with olive oil and season both sides generously with salt and pepper.

4. Heat an outdoor grill or a frying pan over medium heat. Grill or panfry the burgers for approximately 5 to 6 minutes per side (for medium). Sear the burgers while cooking and turn them a quarter turn every couple of minutes. Flip them once, and do not press them.

5. About 1 minute before the burgers are done, place a slice of provolone on top of each patty. When the cheese has begun to melt, remove the burgers and let them rest for 2 to 3 minutes.

6. Build the burgers by first coating the tops and bottoms of the ciabatta rolls liberally with the aioli. Then slide a burger onto the bottom half of each roll, and layer the red peppers, red onions and arugula on top. Cover with the tops of the rolls and serve with your choice of sides. (I like plain old fries!)

Aioli

1 cup mayonnaise

¼ cup sun-dried tomatoes

2 tablespoons kalamata olives

2 tablespoons lemon juice

1 teaspoon olive oil

1 teaspoon minced garlic

¼ teaspoon paprika

Salt and freshly cracked black pepper, to taste

Burgers

1 pound sirloin, cubed large

3 ounces salami (use dry-aged sopressata or your favorite), cubed large

3 ounces prosciutto, chopped

2 ounces cappicola, cubed large

2 tablespoons sliced pepperoncini

1 to 2 cloves garlic, peeled and chopped

½ teaspoon crushed red pepper flakes, or to taste

1 tablespoon olive oil

Salt and freshly ground black pepper, to taste

4 slices provolone cheese

4 ciabatta rolls (or substitute your favorite rolls)

One 12-ounce jar roasted red peppers, cut into wide slices

1 red onion, peeled and sliced thick

1 cup arugula

FOR THE **kiddos**

Shhh! The special meats that go into the burgers are a secret between you and me. Also, make the patties smaller and put them on plain slider buns. I leave off the provolone, red peppers, red onions and arugula and put some simple marinara sauce and a slice of mozzarella (it's milder than provolone) or their favorite burger cheese on top.

Chapter five

REEF RECIPES

Super-serious face

The only fish we had growing up was frozen fish sticks, but they hold a special place in my heart. My mom and I would have fish sticks and fries (also frozen) and watch Graham Kerr's *The Galloping Gourmet* together, followed by *The Carol Burnett Show*. I can't think of fish sticks without remembering those times with my mom. I remember what we were eating and what we were doing thirty-five years ago. Not only is food important for sustenance, but it also helps build our relationships.

Later in life, I ventured into the world of fresh haddock fish-and-chips and created different memories. Being from a long line of Scots, it should be no surprise that my dad was a big fish-and-chips guy. Every couple of weeks we would go out to this dumpy little shop down the road from where we lived and get F & Cs wrapped in newspaper and smothered with malt vinegar. It was heavenly. Crispy batter; flaky, tender fish; and tangy malt vinegar. The outside world didn't exist; it was just me and my dad spending time together. We were never closer than when we shared that meal.

It wasn't until I was in my early twenties that I ate fish that wasn't battered and deep-fried. I tried a pan-seared salmon with a miso–green tea glaze and wasabi served on a bed of fragrant rice. A whole new world just opened up for me. There was so much more out there, and I wanted to start trying new foods and flavors immediately.

I'm hoping this chapter takes you and your family on that same journey. From humble beginnings to a great expanse of cultures, flavors and tastes. Together we will try seafood we've never tried before. The trick is going there by degrees. I was recently talking to somebody who said that she didn't like fish. She said that it seemed so slimy and scaly and that it looked like an "alien." I understand. And that's why I would never try to introduce children or somebody who hasn't had much fish in their life to a whole fish or to one of the more "fishy" fishes. Instead, I'd start with something like a wild salmon or a fresh tuna steak. If you want to get kids on board, it's a good idea to start with dishes that totally disguise the fish itself and slowly introduce the flavors of different fish to the developing palate. Sooner or later, that kid will be more than happy to try other types of fish, just because the first experiences were so good. So c'mon. Let's set sail and discover some great catches the whole family will enjoy.

Maple Syrup and Dijon
ROASTED SALMON

This is a little nod to my Canadian roots. We eat a lot of salmon in the Great White North, but we eat even more maple syrup (and export more of it than any other country in the world). But it's also a nod to my youth, and specifically to a treat I had often as a kid, Sesame Snaps, thin crackers made of sesame seeds and honey. I could have lived on those things. I make my own version with maple syrup, chili pepper and Dijon mustard, an out-of-this-world flavor combination.

SERVES 4 TO 6

1. Line a baking sheet with a nonstick baking mat, such as a Silpat, or with aluminum foil coated with a nonstick cooking spray.

2. Combine all the ingredients for the crackers in a medium heavy saucepan and bring to a boil over high heat, whisking frequently to prevent scorching. Continue cooking, stirring occasionally, until the mixture reaches 280°F, as measured on a candy thermometer.

3. When the sesame-honey mixture is ready, pour it out onto the prepared baking sheet. Spread it evenly with an oiled offset spatula and then allow it to cool on the counter for 45 minutes to 1 hour. Once cool, gently lift up the sesame-honey layer and break it into bite-size pieces. Set aside.

4. Preheat the oven to 425°F.

5. Prepare the glaze for the salmon. Combine the maple syrup, mustard, shallots, scallions and garlic in a blender and process until smooth. Taste and season with salt and pepper. With the blender running, stream in the melted butter. Blend until the butter has been fully incorporated. Pour the glaze into a small shallow bowl and set aside.

6. Prepare the salmon. Line a baking sheet with aluminum foil. Remove any bones from the salmon with needle-nose pliers. Season both sides of the salmon with salt and pepper, to taste, and place the fish, flesh side up, on the prepared baking sheet. Generously brush the salmon with the glaze. Bake for 15 to 20 minutes, or until the flesh flakes with a fork. (It should still be slightly pink in the middle, unless you prefer your salmon well done.)

7. While the salmon is cooking, prepare the garnish. Combine the lime juice, zest and sesame oil in a small bowl and whisk until

Toasted Sesame Crackers

½ cup honey

½ cup toasted sesame seeds

1 teaspoon freshly grated nutmeg

½ teaspoon ground ginger

Salmon

¼ cup maple syrup

3 tablespoons Dijon mustard

1 tablespoon chopped shallots

1 tablespoon chopped scallions

1 clove garlic, peeled

Salt and freshly cracked black pepper, to taste

2 tablespoons unsalted butter, melted

One 1½-pound fresh salmon fillet, center cut (or four 6-ounce fillets)

Garnish

Juice and zest of 1 lime

2 tablespoons sesame oil

6 radishes, ends trimmed and thinly sliced

2 tablespoons chopped fresh dill

2 tablespoons chopped fresh cilantro

2 tablespoons chopped fresh mint

1 tablespoon thinly sliced scallions

1 small serrano chili pepper, seeded and thinly sliced

Salt and freshly cracked black pepper, to taste

completely incorporated. Stir in the radishes, dill, cilantro, mint, scallions and chili pepper. Taste and season with salt and pepper.

8. Serve the salmon with a spoonful of the garnish atop each serving and a scattering of the sesame crackers on each plate.

FOR THE kiddos

Time to play hide that fish! Even though salmon isn't a particularly fishy type of fish, kids just don't seem to take to a plain salmon fillet. It's the color that really throws them off, so I fry them and serve with a dipping sauce. It's called the fish-stick strategy, and I'm cool with it because it still gets them used to the flavor of salmon. You can also bake these strips for a healthier alternative, but make the glaze recipe from the adult version, leaving out the garlic and scallions. Do it right and the kids will never know they're eating that weird, pink, "fishy" salmon that their parents love so much!

½ cup panko bread crumbs

¼ cup cornstarch

2 egg whites

One 6-ounce skinless salmon fillet

¼ to ½ cup canola oil

Salt, to taste

SERVES 2

1 Place the bread crumbs, cornstarch and egg whites in separate small bowls. Whip the egg whites with a fork until foamy.

2 Cut the salmon fillet crosswise into ¼-inch strips. Dip a strip into the cornstarch and lightly coat, shaking off the excess. Then dip it in the egg whites, letting any excess drip off. Finally, dip it in the bread crumbs, patting lightly to make sure they adhere. Place the breaded strip on a clean plate. Repeat until all the strips are breaded. Cover and refrigerate for at least 10 minutes.

3 Meanwhile, heat a ½ inch of oil in a medium cast-iron skillet over medium heat. If the oil bubbles around a wooden spoon dipped in it, you are ready to fry.

4 Carefully slide the salmon strips into the oil and fry until golden and crispy, 1 to 1½ minutes per side. Remove to a paper towel–lined plate. Season with a sprinkling of salt.

5 Serve the strips standing up on a plate or in a small ramekin or bowl, with the dipping sauce of your choice in a separate small bowl to the side. Include a bowl of the sesame crackers from the adult version.

TROUT ALMOND-DEAN

STELLA'S
CHOICE

This was one of the first dishes from culinary school that I made my own. One of the really great things about this dish is that it is simple to put together. The flavors will say you've worked really hard at it, but they'll be lying. Believe me, you don't need to go to culinary school to learn to perfect this dish. Stick with me, and with a little trial and error, in no time you'll be an Almond-Dean master.

SERVES 4

1. Preheat the broiler and place the rack four inches from the top.

2. Place the trout on an oiled baking sheet. Season each fillet with the salt, black pepper, cayenne pepper and a drizzle of olive oil. Broil until cooked through and fish is opaque, about 2 to 4 minutes depending on the size of the fillets. Prick the middle of a fillet with a paring knife or fork and touch the metal to see if it is warm. If it is, the fish is done.

3. While the fish is cooking, heat a heavy sauté pan over medium heat, and melt the butter for the sauce. Add the almonds and shallots, swirling the pan and stirring with a spoon constantly.

4. When the butter starts to brown, add the capers and both citrus juices. Remove the pan from the heat, taste, and season with salt and pepper.

5. Remove the trout from the oven, squeeze lemon over each fillet and sprinkle the lemon zest, parsley and thyme over the fillets. Cover each fillet with a generous amount of sauce and serve.

Fish

- Four 6- to 8-ounce trout fillets
- Olive oil, for oiling the baking sheet and drizzling
- 1 teaspoon salt
- 1 tablespoon freshly ground black pepper
- ¼ teaspoon cayenne pepper
- Zest of 1 lemon (remaining lemon halved lengthwise)
- ½ teaspoon chopped fresh parsley
- 2 teaspoons chopped fresh thyme

Sauce

- ¼ cup unsalted butter, cut into pats
- ½ cup sliced almonds
- 1 tablespoon minced shallots
- 1 tablespoon capers
- 2 tablespoons orange juice
- 1 tablespoon lemon juice
- Salt and freshly ground black pepper, to taste

FOR THE kiddos

I simplify the flavors and bread the fish for that kid-friendly fish-stick texture and appeal. Serve this enough, and believe it or not, they'll eventually graduate to whole fish!

SERVES 2 TO 4

1 Season each trout fillet with salt. Pour the milk and the almond flour in separate small bowls. Dip a fillet in the milk and shake off the excess. Next, dip it in the almond flour, pressing to ensure the flour adheres. Place the coated fillet on a clean plate. Repeat with the second fillet. Let the fillets rest for at least 10 minutes.

2 Heat about ¼ inch of oil in a cast-iron skillet over medium heat. Fry the fillets until golden brown, about 2 minutes per side. Remove to a large paper towel–lined plate.

3 Remove the excess oil from the skillet and sauté the bacon until just crispy. Drain the bacon fat. Add the butter and almonds and cook until the almonds are golden. Remove the skillet from the heat and stir in the lemon juice.

4 Arrange the fillets on each of 2 plates and spoon the bacon-almond sauce over the top. Serve at once.

Two 6-ounce skinless trout fillets, cut into 2-inch squares

Salt, to taste

½ cup whole milk

½ cup coarse almond flour (store-bought or homemade by pulvering raw almonds in a food processor)

¼ to ½ cup canola oil

2 strips bacon, chopped

3 tablespoons unsalted butter, cut into pats

2 tablespoons chopped almonds

1 tablespoon freshly squeezed lemon juice

Sweet-and-Sour
SESAME SHRIMP AND FRIES

If you have a child who will fight you tooth and nail over eating the smallest piece of grilled or baked fish, try shrimp. It's a quick and easy seafood to prepare, and it tastes good almost any way you prepare it. Here you can switch it up by cooking the shrimp in different ways. Crush them into the sesame seeds and deep-fry them, grill them to perfection or lightly sauté them. The shrimp will be delicious no matter what—especially with the crunch of the sesame seeds.

SERVES 4

1. Preheat the oven to 450°F. Line two baking sheets with parchment paper.

2. Prepare the fries. In a large bowl, toss the sweet potato strips with the coconut oil and a pinch of salt. Spread them out on the baking sheets, leaving plenty of room between them. Bake until golden and crispy, 25 to 30 minutes, turning occasionally.

3. While the fries are baking, prepare the shrimp. Butterfly the shrimp by cutting the back of each shrimp from head to the tail with a paring knife. You should cut halfway into the body of the shrimp.

4. In a medium bowl, combine the sesame oil, chili paste, honey and lime zest and mix thoroughly. Add the shrimp to the marinade and toss to coat. Cover and refrigerate for 10 to 20 minutes.

5. Remove the shrimp from the marinade, and reserve the marinade. Let the shrimp air-dry for a few minutes. Gently press down on each shrimp so that the butterflied side opens up.

6. Heat the canola oil in a large heavy sauté pan over medium-high heat. Working in batches, fry the shrimp on both sides until pink, pressing with tongs or a spatula to keep the shrimp flat, about 1 to 1½ minutes per side. Transfer to a plate and set aside.

7. Prepare the sauce. To the same pan, add the garlic and shallots and cook, scraping up the bits left behind by the shrimp, until the garlic browns slightly. Add the green and red bell peppers and the Thai chili pepper, and cook until they begin to brown. Stir in the orange marmalade.

8. When the mixture is sizzling, add the mango and the reserved shrimp marinade. Deglaze the pan with the lime juice and bring the

continued on next page ›››

Fries

4 sweet potatoes, peeled and sliced into ½-inch strips

2 tablespoons coconut oil, melted

Pinch of sea salt

¼ teaspoon cayenne pepper

¼ teaspoon garlic powder

¼ teaspoon chili powder

Shrimp

2 dozen jumbo shrimp, peeled and deveined, with tails on

2 tablespoons sesame oil

1 tablespoon chili paste, or to taste

1 tablespoon honey

Zest of 1 lime

1 tablespoon canola oil

Sauce

2 cloves garlic, peeled and minced

1 shallot, peeled and minced

½ cup chopped green bell pepper

½ cup chopped red bell pepper

2 teaspoons minced red Thai chili peppers

2 tablespoons orange marmalade

½ cup peeled and diced mango

¼ cup lime juice

1 tablespoon sesame oil

Zest of 2 limes

½ cup Thai basil (or substitute purple basil or green basil)

¼ cup minced fresh cilantro, plus ¼ cup for garnish

¼ cup fresh roasted peanuts

2 tablespoons sesame seeds

sauce to a simmer. Return the shrimp to the pan, add the sesame oil, and toss to coat. Next, stir in the basil, ¼ cup of the cilantro, the peanuts and sesame seeds.

9. Remove the fries from the oven once they have finished baking and transfer to a large bowl. Toss with the cayenne pepper, garlic powder and chili powder.

10. To serve, stack the fries in the middle of each of 4 plates, nestle 6 shrimp on top of the fries, drizzle with the sauce and garnish with the remaining ¼ cup cilantro.

FOR THE kiddos

As with other dishes, we're going to pull back on the spiciness and make this more of an eat-with-your-hands type of meal. Instead of the complex and spicy sauce of the adult version, use a simpler dipping sauce combining ½ cup orange marmalade, 1 tablespoon lime juice, 1 tablespoon soy sauce and 2 tablespoons ketchup. Stir it up and then make the shrimp. Butterfly them as you would for the adult version, but dip them in 2 whisked eggs and roll them around in a couple of cups of panko bread crumbs. Fry them up, let them cool and then slide them onto skewers along with orange sections (one of each per skewer) to create a shrimp lollipop! Lean a few shrimp-orange skewers against a pile of the sweet potato fries, put the dipping sauce in a little bowl or ramekin and serve.

SALMON AND TILAPIA GLOBES
with Hollandaise Sauce

Growing up, my mom was the queen of stretching food. This dish is a nod to her skill, using less expensive tilapia to supplement the salmon. Tilapia is a flavor sponge, soaking up the surrounding flavors just like tofu does. You can also use red snapper, grouper or even a fish like tuna. The breaded "globes" are delicately crunchy and I make these bite-size for the kiddos, but otherwise they're good to go!

SERVES 4 TO 6

1. Prepare the fish. Process the salmon and tilapia in a food processor until the texture is fine. Scrape down the sides as you go. Transfer the fish to a medium bowl.

2. Add the capers, cornichons and scallions to the food processor and process until finely minced. Add the caper mixture to the fish and stir to combine.

3. In a small bowl, whisk the egg until frothy. Whisk in the lemon juice and mustard, and then stir the egg mixture into the fish mixture.

4. Prepare the breading. Combine the bread crumbs, dill, parsley, salt and pepper in a medium bowl and mix well. Place the flour in a small bowl. Beat the eggs in a small bowl. Using an ice-cream scoop or your hands, form 3-inch balls from the fish mixture. Gently roll a ball in the flour, dip it in the beaten eggs, and then roll it in the bread crumbs. Place it on a baking sheet. Bread the remaining balls and then refrigerate for 15 to 30 minutes.

5. Prepare the hollandaise sauce. Fill the bottom of a double boiler with 1 inch of water, and bring it to a simmer over medium heat. In the top of the double boiler, combine the egg yolks and a teaspoon of lukewarm water, and whisk gently until the color lightens to a pale yellow. Whisk continuously for about 2 minutes more, or until the yolks thicken.

6. Slowly drizzle in the melted butter, whisking constantly. Remove the top from the double boiler and whisk in the lemon juice, cayenne pepper and salt. Pour the hollandaise into a small bowl, cover and set aside.

7. Heat 1 inch of oil in a large cast-iron skillet over medium heat. If the oil bubbles when you dip a wooden spoon in it, you are ready to fry. Carefully place the breaded globes into the oil, working in batches. Fry until dark golden and crisp, about 4 to 5 minutes per side. Remove to a paper towel–lined plate.

8. Serve the globes at once with hollandaise sauce on the side.

Globes

1 pound boneless, skinless salmon fillets, cut into 2-inch pieces

½ pound boneless, skinless tilapia fillets, cut into 2-inch pieces

1 tablespoon capers

1 tablespoon minced cornichons (or substitute baby dills or another pickle)

1 tablespoon minced scallions

1 large egg

1 tablespoon lemon juice

1 tablespoon whole-grain mustard

1½ to 2 cups canola oil, for frying

Breading

2 cups fresh bread crumbs

1 tablespoon chopped fresh dill

1 tablespoon chopped fresh parsley

Salt and freshly ground black pepper, to taste

1 cup all-purpose flour

3 large eggs

Hollandaise

3 large egg yolks

12 tablespoons unsalted butter, melted

2 teaspoons lemon juice

⅛ teaspoon cayenne pepper

Pinch of salt

FISH-AND-CHIPS
with an Intense Malt Vinegar Reduction

Believe it or not, fish-and-chips are a dish dear to my heart. The only time my father and I really ever managed to get along was over a meal of F & Cs. I couldn't get enough of the one-on-one time with my father—or the fish-and-chips, especially with the malt vinegar. This dish is all about fresh fish, a badass batter and the powerful malt vinegar reduction. The secret ingredient in my batter is a bit of hearty Guinness beer. I think that once you make this simple meal, you're going to want to share it with someone you care about, too.

SERVES 4

1. Prepare the malt vinegar reduction. Heat the vinegar, brown sugar and salt in a small saucepan over medium-high heat and whisk to dissolve the sugar. Bring to a boil, and then reduce the heat and simmer until the liquid is reduced to ½ cup, about 15 minutes. Remove the saucepan from the heat, but leave the malt vinegar reduction in the saucepan.

2. Prepare the fish. Season the fish with salt and black pepper, to taste. Place ½ cup of the flour in a small bowl, and dredge the pieces of fish in the flour one by one. Place the coated fish on a large plate.

3. In a medium bowl, whisk together the remaining flour, baking powder, salt and both peppers. Create a well in the middle of the flour mixture, pour in the beer and egg, and whisk until the batter is smooth.

continued on next page ⟩⟩⟩

Malt Vinegar Reduction

One 12-ounce bottle malt vinegar

½ **cup brown sugar**

½ **teaspoon salt**

Fish

1 **pound cod fillets, cut into finger-size pieces**

½ **cup all-purpose flour, plus 1½ cups for the batter**

1 **teaspoon baking powder**

1½ **teaspoons salt**

½ **teaspoon freshly ground black pepper**

⅛ **teaspoon cayenne pepper**

1½ **cups Guinness beer**

1 **large egg, beaten**

½ **to 1 cup canola oil**

Kosher salt, to taste

FOR THE **kiddos**

Kids are the original fans of anything breaded and fried, so trust me, they'll flip over this dish as is. Although most of the alcohol burns off during frying, I'd suggest you play it safe and eliminate the Guinness from the batter, replacing it with milk (or use club soda for a lighter batter). Dredge, batter and fry the cod as you do with the adult version, but put the malt vinegar reduction in a ramekin for dipping so that the little ones control how much goes on the fish.

4. In a medium cast-iron skillet over medium-high heat, heat about 1 inch of the oil to 350°F. Dip the pieces of cod into the batter, one by one, let the excess batter drip off and then slide them into the skillet. Fry the cod in batches and leave plenty of room around each piece in the skillet. Fry the fish until golden, 2 to 3 minutes per side, and remove to a paper towel–lined plate.

5. Place the fried cod in a large bowl and add a large spoonful of the malt vinegar reduction. Toss gently, ensuring that the cod pieces are well coated, and then arrange them on each of 4 plates. Drizzle the remaining reduction over the top and sprinkle with the kosher salt before serving with the chips.

Dean's Food 411
THE CHIPS

It's fun to make your own "chips" for this dish, and they taste better. But if you're pressed for time, you can buy a bag of quality frozen French fries and use one of these ideas to make them unique. But just this one time.

★ Grate about ½ cup Parmesan cheese (or your little ones' favorite cheese) and toss it with the still-hot fries. Place the fries under the broiler and melt the cheese for a super treat!

★ Mix equal parts ketchup and mayo and season with a pinch of pepper for an easy dip! It's a Canadian thing. You'll love it.

★ Combine ½ cup each of mayonnaise, sour cream and buttermilk with 1 tablespoon each of lemon juice and champagne vinegar. Whisk together and serve with the fries.

★ Try a BBQ angle by mixing together 1 tablespoon each of brown sugar and paprika, 1 teaspoon each of black pepper, chili powder, garlic powder and onion powder, and ½ teaspoon cayenne pepper. Thoroughly blend, taste and add salt, if desired. Sprinkle over the hot fries.

★ Go fancy by seasoning the hot fries with truffle salt. People won't believe you didn't slave away in the kitchen, slicing and frying these potatoes by hand.

CRAB- AND SHRIMP-STUFFED BREAM
with Lemon-Butter Sauce

Of all my adventures in the fish world, this is one of the most elegant and impressive. It practically screams gourmet. And as impressive as it seems, it's really not a hard dish to make. And the sauce is perfect for just about any white fish or even chicken. You can also modify the recipe, using smaller snappers to create a stunning date-night feast.

SERVES 4

1. Slice the fish along its belly and thoroughly clean it, removing all internal organs. Scale the fish and wash it thoroughly. (Or have the fish shop or counter do all this for you.) Pat dry with paper towels inside and out and refrigerate.

2. Preheat the oven to 350°F or heat the grill over medium-high heat. (Grilling will give the fish a smokier, richer flavor.)

3. Melt the butter in a medium saucepan over medium heat. Sauté the onions, carrots and bell peppers for about 2 minutes, or until soft. Add the scallions, garlic and jalapeño and continue to sauté for about 1 minute.

4. Add the shrimp, ginger, cumin, coriander, salt and pepper, and toss. Cook until the shrimp are pink and tender, about 5 minutes.

5. Remove the saucepan from the heat and let it cool slightly before adding the crackers, crab, parsley, lime juice and zest. Toss to combine.

6. Lay the fish on a baking sheet and gently score the top, making five diagonal lines (cut just through the skin). Season with salt and pepper and drizzle with olive oil, gently massaging the seasonings into the cuts. Stuff the fish with the shrimp-crab mixture, and top with the parsley sprigs and lemon slices.

7. Bake for 10 minutes per pound, or about 40 minutes for a 4-pound fish. Do not overcook. When the fish is properly cooked, the flesh should flake with a fork.

8. While the fish is cooking, prepare the sauce. Cook the wine in a medium saucepan over high heat until it is reduced by half. Add the lemon juice. Then add the butter, one pat at a time, whisking constantly. Let the sauce come to a low boil between each pat.

9. Remove the saucepan from the heat and stir in the parsley, salt and pepper. Serve the baked fish on a large platter and cover with the sauce. This is served family style, so dig in and watch for bones.

Fish

One whole 4-pound bream or roughy

2½ tablespoons unsalted butter

½ cup minced white onions

½ carrot, peeled and minced

2 tablespoons minced green bell pepper

2 scallions, root ends removed and thinly sliced

2 small cloves garlic, peeled and minced

¼ jalapeño pepper, seeded and minced

¼ pound 16/20 shrimp, peeled, deveined and diced

1 tablespoon grated fresh ginger

¼ teaspoon fresh ground cumin

⅛ teaspoon ground coriander

Salt and freshly ground black pepper, to taste

2 cups crushed oyster crackers

½ pound fresh lump crabmeat

1 tablespoon chopped fresh parsley, plus 2 sprigs for baking the fish

Juice and zest of 1 small lime

1 tablespoon olive oil, for drizzling

3 slices lemon

Sauce

½ cup dry white wine

4 tablespoons lemon juice

4 tablespoons unsalted butter, cut into pats

2 tablespoons chopped fresh parsley

½ teaspoon salt

Freshly cracked black pepper, to taste

CRUNCHY SALMON BURGERS
with Lemon and Tarragon

If you've ever had a well-made salmon burger, you know how great they can be. It's hard to come up with the right formula to make them hold together well and not dry out. If you're going to make the effort—especially if you're going to turn your kids on to the beauty of a salmon burger at its best—you need to pack it full of flavor, keep it moist and finish it with just a little mayo or homemade aioli.

SERVES 4

1. Process the salmon in a food processor until coarsely ground (scraping down the sides as necessary). Transfer the salmon to a large bowl. Add the bread crumbs, scallions, egg, lemon juice and lemon zest, mustard, tarragon, dill, garlic, salt and pepper, and mix until all the ingredients are incorporated.

2. With a 3- to 4-inch ring cutter, form the salmon mixture into patties. Place the ring cutter on a plate, pack the salmon mixture into it and then gently remove the ring cutter. Place the patty on a clean plate. Repeat until all the patties are formed.

3. Preheat a large cast-iron skillet over high heat for 2 minutes. Add 1½ tablespoons of the canola oil and 1 tablespoon of the butter to the skillet. Add half the patties to the skillet and cook on both sides until they have a crispy golden coating, about 4 minutes per side. Reduce the heat to medium and cook for about 2 minutes more per side, or until the patties are cooked through. Remove them to a clean plate. Cook the second batch the same way in the remaining 1½ tablespoons canola oil and 1 tablespoon butter.

4. Serve the salmon burgers on toasted, buttered brioche buns and top with mayo (or the aioli on page 102) and your choice of condiments.

1½ pounds boneless, skinless salmon fillets or steaks, cut into 2-inch pieces

¾ cup panko bread crumbs

2 scallions, root ends removed and finely sliced

1 large egg, slightly beaten

Juice and zest of ½ small lemon

1 tablespoon Dijon mustard

2 teaspoons minced fresh tarragon

3 teaspoons chopped dill

1 clove garlic, minced

1 teaspoon salt

½ teaspoon freshly cracked black pepper

3 tablespoons canola oil, divided

2 tablespoons unsalted butter, divided

4 brioche buns, sliced, buttered and toasted

FOR THE **kiddos**

Follow the instructions for the adult version, but run all the "green stuff" through the food processor with the salmon. This helps disguise it. I also kid-size the burgers, making sliders rather than normal-size patties. Cut the brioche buns or your kids' favorite burger buns down to slider size to keep them happy and wolfing down the Super Salmon Sliders.

WHOLE ROASTED SNAPPER
Dragged through the Garden

If you've never prepared a whole fish, it's time to step up your game. In my experience, people are often intimidated by preparing a fish head to tail, but the Gourmet Dad isn't going to let you back away from this challenge. Cooking fish whole makes for an incredibly dramatic presentation at the table, but more importantly, it's a great way to keep the flesh moist and saturated with flavors. And there are a lot of flavors going on in this dish. I've included just about every vegetable you can imagine here, plus a boatload of aromatic herbs. Pick a fish as fresh as possible. (Fresh whole fish won't smell like fish at all; it should smell like the sea, and the eyes should be nice and clear.) The recipe here calls for two whole snappers because the smaller fish are more widely available. But you can substitute a single 4-pound fish for an even more dramatic presentation.

SERVES 4

1. Preheat a charcoal grill over medium-high heat. A charcoal grill is preferable, but if you have a gas grill, that will work as well.

2. Slice the fish along its belly and thoroughly clean it, removing all internal organs. Scale the fish and wash it thoroughly (or have the fish shop or counter do all this for you). Pat dry with paper towels inside and out. Lightly score each fish, making 3 to 4 diagonal shallow cuts on each side. Season the fish generously with salt and pepper on both sides and inside the fish.

3. Heat the canola oil and butter in a large skillet over medium heat. Add the celery, fennel, onions and leeks and sauté for 5 minutes. Add the scallions and garlic, and sauté for 1 minute. Season with salt and pepper. Let cool briefly.

4. Stuff each fish with half the vegetable mixture, and then generously brush olive oil over them. Top each fish with 4 to 5 lemon wheels and 1 sprig of each herb. Refrigerate for 20 to 30 minutes, or until your grill is ready.

5. Put each fish in an oiled fish basket and then place them on the grill. Cover each with 1 more sprig of each herb. Grill the fish over evenly spread coals (or over even, direct gas heat if you are using a gas grill), rotating occasionally and turning once. Cook for 10 to 15 minutes per side. Serve garnished with the remaining herb sprigs.

Two 1½- to 2-pound whole red snappers

Salt and freshly cracked black pepper, to taste

1 tablespoon canola oil

1 tablespoon unsalted butter

2 medium celery stalks, thinly sliced

1 small fennel bulb, stem trimmed and thinly sliced

½ cup thinly sliced red onions

¼ cup julienned leeks (white part only)

4 scallions (green part only), root ends removed and cut diagonally into thin slices

2 cloves garlic, peeled and sliced

2 tablespoons olive oil for brushing

2 lemons, sliced into thin wheels

6 sprigs each fresh mint, fresh parsley, fresh thyme, fresh dill

 FOR THE **kiddos**

You can use this recipe as is, but dial back on the spiciness by leaving out the chili powder, garlic and jalapeño. There are all kinds of things you can do to this one to spruce it up for the little ones. Aside from using their favorite cheeses, you can go wild with the topping. Crush up Cheez-It® crackers for the topping (watch carefully because they burn quickly) or mix different flavors of potato chips, and let the kids crush up the chips. You can make it a little more special by baking individual servings in small casseroles.

MY MOM'S TUNA CASSEROLE

STELLA'S CHOICE

I can't talk about comfort food without talking about my mom's tuna casserole. It was one of her best recipes, probably because it was one of the simplest. But the one thing she left off was a crispy, crunchy crust. You can substitute whatever cheese tickles your fancy, and the same goes for the pasta. I love the flavor and texture of egg noodles, but you can easily go with your kids' favorite. Put your own signature on the crust, as well. I keep it simple with tortilla chips, but I'm just as likely to mix it up with jalapeño chips (a Canadian favorite) for a little extra kick, or even salt and vinegar chips, to add some tangy flavor.

SERVES 4 TO 6

1. Preheat the oven to 450°F.

2. Bring a large pot three-quarters full of salted water to a boil over high heat. Add the noodles and cook them until they are al dente. Drain, rinse with cold water, drain again and return the noodles to the pot.

3. Heat the oil in a medium pot over medium heat, and sauté the onions, scallions, jalapeños and garlic until tender, about 4 minutes. Add the mushrooms and cook until slightly wilted, 1 to 2 minutes. Add the ancho chili powder, salt and pepper.

4. Pour in the cream of mushroom soup, and then fill the empty can half full of water, stir and add that to the pot. Bring the mixture to a gentle simmer, stirring frequently to prevent burning. Add the tuna, ½ cup of the cheddar cheese and ½ cup of the pepper jack cheese, and stir to melt the cheese.

5. Once the cheese has melted, add the tuna mixture into the noodles. Mix in the crème fraîche and chives, combining well.

6. Pour the tuna-noodle mixture into an oiled 9 x 13-inch baking dish. Top with the remaining ½ cup cheddar, the remaining ½ cup pepper jack and the crushed chips. Bake for 10 to 15 minutes, or until the cheese has melted and the casserole is warm in the center.

One 12-ounce package egg noodles

2 tablespoons olive oil

½ cup chopped yellow onion

2 scallions, root ends removed and chopped

2 tablespoons minced jalapeño pepper

1 clove garlic, peeled and minced

1 cup sliced button mushrooms

½ teaspoon ancho chili powder

Salt and freshly ground black pepper, to taste

One 10-ounce can cream of mushroom soup

Two 6-ounce cans chunk white tuna, drained

½ cup shredded sharp cheddar cheese, plus ½ cup for topping

½ cup shredded pepper jack cheese, plus ½ cup for topping

½ cup crème fraîche

1 tablespoon chopped fresh chives

1½ cups crushed tortilla chips (or substitute a favorite chip)

California Coast
SALMON SURFBOARDS

This was my first signature Gourmet Dad dish. It's a simple dish, basically just breaded salmon strips with mashed potatoes and beans. But the spin I put on it for the kids launched the Gourmet Dad idea. Since kids can be a little iffy with salmon, I made glorified fish sticks and turned them into surfboards riding a "wave" of purple potatoes with green bean "rocks." It's still one of the most fun dishes I make for my kids, and to be honest, adults like the kid version almost as much as the kids do.

SERVES 4

4 russet potatoes, peeled and quartered

½ cup half-and-half

4 tablespoons unsalted butter, plus 1 tablespoon for sautéing the beans

1 teaspoon salt, divided

1 teaspoon white pepper, divided

¾ cup panko bread crumbs

¾ cup self-rising flour

2 large eggs

¼ cup whole milk

Two 8-ounce skinless salmon fillets, pinbones removed and cut into ½-inch strips

½ cup vegetable oil

2 cups green beans, ends trimmed and cut into ¼-inch pieces

1. Boil the potatoes in a large pot filled halfway with salted water. When the potatoes are fork-tender, turn off the heat, drain the potatoes, and return them to the pot on the burner.

2. Combine the half-and-half and 4 tablespoons of the butter in a small pot and bring to a boil over medium-high heat, stirring frequently. Remove from the heat the second it starts to boil.

3. Mash the potatoes with a masher or hand mixer. (Do not overwork them or they'll become thick and pasty.) Slowly fold in the hot butter mixture and half the salt and pepper. Taste and adjust the seasonings as desired.

4. Transfer the potatoes to the top of a double boiler. Add water to the bottom, heat it to a simmer, and then put the mashed potatoes on top, covered, to stay warm.

5. Place the bread crumbs in a small bowl. Mix together the flour and the remaining salt and pepper in a second small bowl. Combine the eggs and milk in a third small bowl and mix well.

6. Dredge a salmon strip in the flour and shake off any excess. Next, dip it into the egg wash, and let the excess drain off. Finally, press it into the bread crumbs, and shake off any excess. Place the breaded salmon strip on a plate. Repeat until all the salmon strips are breaded.

7. Heat the oil in a large frying pan over medium-high heat. Fry the salmon strips in batches. Slide some salmon strips into the hot oil, one by one, and fry for 2 to 3 minutes per side, or until golden brown. Remove to a paper towel–lined plate. Repeat until all the salmon strips have been fried.

8. Heat the butter in another large skillet over medium heat and sauté the green beans, stirring occasionally, until slightly withered and browned. Add a pinch of salt, if desired, to the beans, toss and remove from the heat.

9. Serve the fried salmon with a heaping serving of the potatoes and the green beans alongside. Or transform the salmon into surf-boards hanging ten on potato waves (see "For the Kiddos" below) for adults and kids alike.

FOR THE kiddos

If you want kids to dive into their food, it's a good idea to make something they can actually dive into! Mimic the ocean by using purple potatoes. When everything is ready to serve, form a wave with the potatoes by shaping them into a long triangle on the plate and folding the tip over to look like a wave curl. Put the salmon "surfboards" on the wave, and spread the green beans in front of the wave in such a way that they look like rocks. Cowabunga, you're done!

Chapter six

DEANO'S ITALIANO

Man, I love pasta! Well, I love Italian food, period, but pasta is my favorite because there are so many ways to prepare it. And growing up, it was a lifesaver in my mother's kitchen. One of my favorite pasta dishes as a kid was…now, don't laugh…canned spaghetti on hot buttered toast. I would run home from grade school at lunch, just to get a big plate of this masterpiece. The tangy sauce, the mushy noodles and the butter-laden toast all came together to create a magical dish that made me happy.

But it was one of my mom's signature dishes that I couldn't get enough of—spaghetti with meatballs. Pasta started out as Italian peasant food for good reason: a small amount can stretch to feed a lot of hungry mouths. My mom used to load up those meatballs with a healthy helping of crackers, making the meat go a lot further than it normally would have, but they were still the stuff of perfect childhood memories. Many a happy meal was had at our kitchen table, clustered around that spaghetti and meatballs. And at its heart, that's what pasta is all about, too—simple, good food that fills you up, gives your taste buds something to celebrate and makes for perfect social occasions.

My dad was fond of saying, "Keep it simple, stupid," and I think that is right on the money when it comes to pasta. There's no need to overcomplicate this type of cooking. In my mind, there's just nothing better than properly cooked linguini with a fresh tomato-basil sauce.

I kept that in mind when I came up with the recipes in this chapter. They all focus on fresh, wholesome flavors from basic spices and simple combinations. Throw together a few fresh ingredients and you can make a world-class meal.

One thing I strongly recommend if you want to get the most out of your pasta is to make it yourself. Homemade pasta is really a different experience, and it's not difficult. Don't get me wrong. I love store-bought dried pasta. But if you have the time, making your own pasta is fun and therapeutic. I zone out while I'm kneading the dough, drifting off to a little piazza in Sicily. I daydream that I'm hanging the pasta to dry in the window of my restaurant, La Dolce Deano's, as hungry patrons line up outside for the dinner service. Ah, how great that would be.

You may not be able to start your own Italian trattoria, but you can turn your kitchen into a *cucina* by making your own rigatoni, penne, gnocchi, red sauces and pestos. All the recipes that follow are versatile, so you can change them to suit your own tastes. They're all fun and inexpensive, and most can be frozen for meals throughout the week. Get the kids involved, and you'll have just as much fun creating the meal as you'll have eating it.

QUICK TOMATO SAUCE

Every cook should have a simple tomato sauce in his or her back pocket. It can be used on all kinds of pastas, over rice and even to liven up vegetables, like broccoli or carrots. This one is easy to make and takes no time at all—it's a great weeknight option. This version will make 6⅔ cups, enough for several meals, and it freezes well.

Two 28-ounce cans peeled whole San Marzano tomatoes

¼ cup olive oil

4 cloves garlic, peeled

1 yellow onion, peeled and diced

2 tablespoons tomato paste

1 to 2 teaspoons crushed red pepper flakes, or to taste

Salt and freshly cracked black pepper, to taste

6 sprigs fresh basil

1. Pour the tomatoes into a large bowl and squeeze them to break them up into small pieces.

2. Heat the olive oil in a medium saucepot over medium-high heat. Add the garlic cloves and sauté until golden brown, about 3 minutes. Add the onions and cook until caramelized, 8 to 10 minutes.

3. Stir in the tomato paste and the red pepper flakes (if you want to add spiciness). Add the tomatoes with their juice and then season with salt and pepper. Bring the sauce to a boil and add the basil sprigs. Lower the heat and simmer the sauce until you're ready to serve. Discard the basil sprigs and the garlic cloves before serving.

Dean's Food 411

Here's the lowdown on one of those basic kitchen techniques that seem to trip people up all the time in their kitchens: cooking perfect pasta. It starts with the water. You want six quarts at least to cook a pound of pasta (that's a gallon and a half). The more water, the better because it helps dilute the starch coming off the pasta. And salt is crucial: the water should be "as salty as the sea." The salt will prevent the pasta from sticking together. (Never, ever, never add oil to pasta water.)

The ideal pasta is cooked al dente, which is Italian for "to the tooth." It means that there is a slight crunch or resistance when you bite into the pasta. The only way you can determine doneness is to test the pasta during the cooking process.

The traditional Italian way to prepare a sauced pasta is to drain it, return it to the pot, add a ladle of sauce and toss to coat. This helps saturate the pasta with the flavors of the sauce. Then you can add the rest of the sauce. Or my favorite is to add your pasta that is not quite al dente to your hot sauce that has been cooking for a while, and finish cooking your pasta in the sauce. Word of caution: Another common mistake people make with pasta is drowning it in sauce. You need only enough to coat the noodles thoroughly. All the flavors will be there, and you won't have a swimming pool of sauce left over on the plate.

PASTA ALLA CHECCA (TORI'S FAVORITE)

STELLA'S CHOICE

Tori loves it when I make this classic pasta dish. It's light, refreshing and full of flavor, so what's not to love? This is a traditional summer pasta meant to include ingredients right out of the garden. Tomatoes, fresh herbs and simple spices combine with a touch of cheese to make for a sparkling dish that is perfect anytime, anywhere. I've kept my version as simple as possible to honor the idea of the original. This comes together quickly and is delicious and memorable for the whole family. Go even more authentic and fresh with raw skinned tomatoes if your preferences run a bit more rustic.

SERVES 4

1. Bring a large pot of water to a boil over high heat. While the water is heating, remove the stem from the tomatoes and cut a small *X* on the *bottom* of each with a paring knife. Prepare a large bowl three-quarters full of ice and add water to fill.

2. Drop the tomatoes in the boiling water and reduce to a simmer. Cook the tomatoes for 30 to 60 seconds, or until the skins at the *X* start to pull back.

3. Gently remove the tomatoes with a slotted spoon and place them in the ice bath. Once the tomatoes are completely chilled, remove and peel the skin from each.

4. Quarter each tomato, remove and discard the seeds and any hard core, and finely dice the tomatoes.

5. Heat the oil in a very large skillet over medium-high heat. Add the garlic and sauté for 30 seconds, stirring constantly. Add the red pepper flakes and cook until the garlic starts to brown slightly.

6. Next, add the tomatoes, oregano, pepper and salt. Add the cooked linguini, stirring to coat, and then remove the skillet from the heat.

7. Fold in the Parmigiano-Reggiano and the basil. When the cheese has melted, serve the linguini in warm pasta bowls and top each with a small chunk of burrata.

2 pounds plum tomatoes

¼ cup extra-virgin olive oil

1 tablespoon minced garlic

1 to 2 teaspoons crushed red pepper flakes, or to taste

2 sprigs fresh oregano, leaves only, chopped

2 teaspoons freshly cracked black pepper

Salt, to taste

1 pound linguini, cooked al dente (or substitute spaghetti, angel hair or bucatini)

2 tablespoons fresh grated Parmigiano-Reggiano cheese

8 to 12 fresh basil leaves, slivered

4 ounces fresh burrata, cut into 1-inch pieces (or substitute mozzarella pearls)

FOR THE kiddos

This is such a simple dish that it's good to go for the little ones with just a couple of tweaks. Go easy on the garlic and lose the red pepper flakes. For some crunch, I cut a baguette diagonally into slices, brush the slices with olive oil, season them with salt and pepper, and top them with shredded Parmesan. I then toast the slices in an oven or toaster oven set at 350°F for 8 to 10 minutes, or until golden brown.

Dean's
SUNDAY GRAVY

If you don't have an Italian grandmother, you might not know about Sunday Gravy. Italian immigrants usually made the sauce in a huge batch on Sunday for the traditional end-of-the-week pasta dinner. It was the height of simplicity, based on meat, tomatoes and a few traditional spices, but it was rich and filling. The idea was to make a huge batch so that the extra could be saved for meals during the week. I grew up in an Italian neighborhood and learned about Sunday Gravy from a friend's mom. She'd start it in the morning, let it simmer all day, and then, come dinnertime, she'd throw a little pasta in water and, boom, dinner was ready. You can use this rich, meaty sauce over your favorite pasta or even on rice. But I suggest you consider doubling or even tripling the recipe, because this is just about the greatest leftover meal you'll ever have.

SERVES 6 TO 8

1 rack pork ribs, cut into 3-rib sections

1½ pounds boneless pork shoulder, cut into 2 pieces

Salt and freshly cracked black pepper, to taste

3 tablespoons olive oil, plus 5 tablespoons for the garlic

1½ pounds spicy Italian link sausage, casings removed and crumbled

4 cloves garlic, peeled and smashed

Five 28-ounce cans peeled whole San Marzano tomatoes

2 cups full-bodied red wine (preferably Cabernet Sauvignon or Zinfandel)

1. Season the ribs and the pork shoulder generously with salt and pepper and brush with 3 tablespoons of the oil. Heat a large pot over high heat until it is nearly smoking. Brown the ribs and pork shoulder in batches, about 10 to 12 minutes per batch. In a large sauté pan over medium-high heat, brown the sausage. Remove all the meat to a large plate and set aside.

2. Reduce the heat for the pot to medium, pour the remaining 5 tablespoons oil into the pot, add the garlic and brown it for 1 to 1½ minutes, almost frying it. Remove the garlic and discard.

3. Pour the tomatoes into a large bowl in batches and squeeze them to break them up into small pieces. Add half of the tomatoes to the pot (be careful, as it will splatter), pour in the wine and bring to a boil. Reduce the heat and simmer, stirring occasionally, until the liquid is reduced by half, about 15 to 20 minutes.

4. Add the meat and the remaining tomatoes to the pot. Bring to a boil over medium heat, and then reduce the heat and simmer, uncovered, until the meat is tender and the ribs are falling off the bone, about 3 hours. Stir occasionally. Remove the bones and discard.

5. Taste and season the sauce with salt and pepper, if desired. Serve the meat as is or shred it. Don't strain the sauce. Keep it chunky, or make it smoother by pulsing it in a blender or food processor or with an immersion blender. Serve the sauce with your favorite pasta.

Dean's Food 411

Sunday Gravy is perfect for now and later. If you've made extra, allow it to cool to room temperature, and then divvy it up between single-serving (or larger) containers. Refrigerate any that you expect to use in the next day or two. Otherwise, freeze the extra. It will keep for up to a month or more in the freezer without losing flavor.

A recipe doesn't have to be complicated to be truly great, as this dish proves. I can't tell you how much I loved this meal growing up. *Everyone* in the family loved my mom's spaghetti and meatballs. She would mix in crushed crackers to stretch the meat, but I do it to add a little texture and help the meatballs hold together better. Also, the crackers enable the meatballs to soak up sauce and flavor. I also use both pork and beef in my version, which creates an incredible texture and mix of flavors. Dress the pasta with Dean's Sunday Gravy (page 134) to really add to the meatiness of the dish, or you can use Quick Tomato Sauce (page 132), a lighter and simpler tomato sauce. Or just use your favorite jarred sauce. The meatballs won't mind, and they'll stand up to just about any red sauce you might want to use.

SERVES 4 TO 6

1. Preheat the oven to 400°F.

2. Heat the oil in a medium sauté pan over medium-high heat. Add the celery, carrots, onions and garlic to the pan and sauté until tender. Set aside and let cool.

3. In a large bowl, combine the vegetable mixture, the pork, beef, crackers, eggs, Parmigiano-Reggiano, fontina, parsley, basil, salt and pepper. Mix with your hands until all the ingredients are incorporated, but do not overwork the mixture. (Overworking could result in dry and tough meatballs.)

4. Form 2-inch meatballs from the meat mixture with an ice-cream scoop. Space the meatballs out evenly on a baking sheet. Bake, turning once midway through cooking, until golden brown, about 10 minutes per side.

5. Transfer the browned meatballs to a stockpot. Add the Sunday Gravy (or tomato sauce) and the beef stock, and bring just to a boil over medium heat. Lower the heat and simmer, allowing the meatballs to cook through, for about 15 minutes. Serve over the spaghetti and garnish with the remaining 2 teaspoons Parmigiano-Reggiano.

2 tablespoons olive oil

2 celery stalks, minced

2 carrots, peeled and minced

1 yellow onion, peeled and minced

2 large cloves garlic, peeled and minced

1 pound ground pork

1 pound ground beef

2 cups finely crushed saltine crackers

2 large eggs, lightly beaten

½ cup finely grated Parmigiano-Reggiano cheese, plus 2 teaspoons for garnish

¼ cup finely grated fontina

2 tablespoons chopped fresh parsley

2 tablespoons chopped fresh basil

Salt and pepper, to taste

4 cups Dean's Sunday Gravy (page 134) or Quick Tomato Sauce (page 132) or jarred sauce

1½ cups beef stock

1 pound spaghetti, cooked al dente

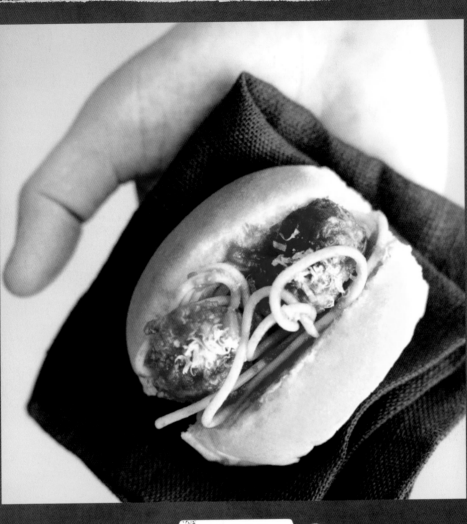

FOR THE **kiddos**

If you want to fill your kitchen with extra helpings of giggles, just get your children involved in making meatballs. My kids smush all the ingredients together with their hands, which they think is the funniest thing. Just don't allow them to over-knead the meat mixture, or the meatballs become tough. I also give my kids a melon baller to make the meatballs bite-size, and sometimes we put them on skewers before cooking. And even though kids love slurping spaghetti with their meatballs, you can throw together meatball sammies made with mini dinner rolls or slider buns. Slather them up with sauce, melt a little cheese over the top

THREE-MEAT LASAGNA

I like lasagna as much as the next guy, but I've found that it can sometimes be a little boring, and it's prone to falling apart when you cut it. I always make sure to drain my ricotta, to give the lasagna a fluffier texture and ensure against a fall-apart mess, and I use three types of meat. Another secret is using no-boil lasagna noodles. Just layer them dry and they'll cook with the rest of the ingredients—soaking up a lot of that meaty goodness and super-delicious herb mix in the process.

SERVES 6

1. Preheat the oven to 375°F.

2. Drain the ricotta by wrapping it in cheesecloth or spooning it into a large coffee filter, placing it in a mesh strainer over a large bowl and refrigerating for at least 2 hours. (You can do this the night before.)

3. Prepare the sauce. Heat a very large pan over medium-high heat. Add the ground beef and pork and cook it, breaking the meat up with a wooden spoon, until it has browned, about 8 minutes. Remove the meat to a large plate and set aside.

4. Drain the excess fat from the skillet and sauté the onions until tender, about 4 minutes. Reduce the heat to medium, add the garlic, and cook, stirring, for 1 minute. Return the meat to the skillet. Add the tomato sauce and oregano and bring to a boil. Reduce the heat and simmer for 30 minutes, stirring occasionally.

5. While the sauce is cooking, mix together the drained ricotta, ½ cup of the Parmesan, the eggs, parsley, thyme, lemon zest, salt and pepper in a large bowl.

6. Coat a deep 9 x 13-inch baking dish with the oil. Spread a thin layer of sauce on the bottom of the dish. Place 3 noodles in a single layer atop the sauce, and top these with one-third of the ricotta mixture, one-quarter of the chorizo, ⅓ cup of the remaining Parmesan, 1 cup of the mozzarella and a generous ladle of sauce.

7. Spread the basil evenly across the top. Repeat this process to form two layers topped with a layer of noodles. Finish with the last of the sauce and the remaining chorizo.

Two 16-ounce containers ricotta cheese

1 pound freshly ground chuck beef

1 pound freshly ground pork

1 cup finely diced onion

2 cloves garlic, peeled and minced

4 cups Quick Tomato Sauce (page 132)

2 tablespoons chopped fresh oregano

½ cup shredded Parmesan cheese, plus 1 cup for the layers

2 large eggs

2 tablespoons chopped fresh parsley

2 tablespoons chopped fresh thyme

Zest of 1 lemon

Salt and freshly ground black pepper, to taste

Olive oil, for coating the baking dish

9 large no-boil lasagna noodles (found at your local supermarket)

1 pound Spanish chorizo, thinly sliced

3 cups shredded mozzarella, plus ½ cup for topping

¼ cup slivered fresh basil leaves

continued on next page ›››

8. Place the lasagna on a baking sheet. Cover tightly with foil and bake for 60 minutes. Carefully remove the lasagna from the oven, take off the foil and sprinkle the remaining ½ cup mozzarella on top. Return the lasagna to the oven and bake, uncovered, for 15 minutes more, or until golden brown and bubbly.

9. Carefully remove the lasagna from the oven, loosely tent with foil and let stand for 20 minutes before serving.

FOR THE **kiddos**

You know what kids love even better than lasagna? Lasagna cupcakes! We sub the noodles for cooked wonton wrappers and use less meat, and the kiddos just gobble them up. You can even place a candle in one of the cupcakes for a birthday dinner.

SERVES 4

12 wonton wrappers

1 cup sauce (from adult recipe)

¾ cup ricotta mixture (from adult recipe)

1¼ cups Parmesan cheese

8 slices pepperoni

1 Preheat the oven to 375°F. Spray 4 of the wells of a muffin tin with nonstick spray.

2 Cut circles out of the wonton wrappers using a 2-inch biscuit cutter. Press the wonton wrapper circles into the 4 wells of the prepared muffin tin.

3 Cover the wonton wrapper layer with 1 tablespoon sauce, 1 tablespoon ricotta mixture and 1 tablespoon Parmesan, in that order. Repeat to make three layers. Add a final layer of sauce and sprinkle each with 1½ tablespoons Parmesan. Top each with 2 pepperoni slices.

4 Place the muffin tin on a baking sheet. Bake for 30 minutes, or until the pepperoni is crispy and the cheese is browned and bubbly. Use a small spatula to remove the lasagna cupcakes from the muffin tin. Let them cool for 10 minutes before serving.

Spicy Tomato and Zucchini ORECCHIETTE

I'm going to admit up front that I have a fascination with different pastas. Who can blame me? There are more than a hundred types from Southern Italy alone! Sometimes I'll even build a dish around a particular type of pasta. The one I use in this recipe translates from the Italian *orecchio,* or small ears. But because of the shape, they are big flavor traps. I use them to grab hold of the rich, spicy tomato-ness of the sauce, along with the mix of fresh herbs and the dash of cheese. It's as super delicious as it is pretty, easy and quick to make.

SERVES 4 TO 6

1. Heat a large sauté pan over high heat. Add 2 tablespoons oil and toss the zucchini in the oil. Cook until it browns, 2 to 3 minutes. Add the shallots and garlic (and a little more oil, if necessary, because the zucchini tends to absorb it), and sauté until golden, about 2 minutes.

2. Add the tomatoes, oregano and parsley. Use a wooden spoon to scrape up any bits stuck to the pan. Then stir in the red pepper flakes, paprika, salt and pepper, and let the sauce simmer for 5 minutes.

3. Add the cooked orecchiette, the remaining 2 tablespoons oil, 2 tablespoons of the Romano cheese and 4 of the basil leaves.

4. Serve the orecchiette in warm bowls and garnish with the remaining 2 tablespoons Romano and 4 basil leaves.

- 2 tablespoons olive oil, plus 2 tablespoons added with the pasta
- 3 zucchini, ends trimmed and finely diced
- ¼ cup diced shallots
- 2 cloves garlic, peeled and minced
- 2 cups chopped heirloom tomatoes (or substitute Roma or vine-ripened)
- 2 tablespoons chopped fresh oregano
- 1 tablespoon chopped fresh parsley
- 1 teaspoon crushed red pepper flakes
- 1 teaspoon smoked paprika
- Salt and freshly cracked black pepper, to taste
- 1 pound orecchiette, cooked al dente
- 2 tablespoons finely grated Romano cheese, plus 2 tablespoons for garnish
- 4 torn fresh basil leaves, plus 4 for garnish

FOR THE **kiddos**

Pull back on the spices by half, or eliminate them altogether. Want a surefire way to success with this one? Toss the pasta with about ½ cup diced fresh mozzarella, and bake in a 400°F oven until golden and bubbly. It's a perfect alternative to mac and cheese!

Dean's Food 411

This is a simple dish, and the zucchini has a simple flavor. Mix it up a little bit by grilling the zucchini. Cut the zucchini into ¼-inch-thick slices. Fire up the grill or a grill pan and coat the slices with olive oil. Season with a sprinkling of parsley, oregano, salt and pepper. Grill them until golden, about 4 minutes per side. Let them cool and dice them small. It's a great way to add a little bump of smoky flavor—even in salads!

BAKED ZITI
with Boar Sausage

You know baked ziti, and you like it fine. But it's never knocked your socks off. That's because you've never had Deano's baked ziti. Anybody who has seen me ride a motorcycle knows that I'm not fond of anything boring. And sometimes, let's face it, baked ziti is just boring. Not this ziti. My ziti is made with wild boar sausage, some unusual, high-impact spices and three distinctly different cheeses. But the dish really centers on the wild boar sausage, which I love, and the flavor really shines in this dish. Boar has become much more widely available in the past decade, but if you have trouble finding it, you can always substitute your favorite spicy Italian sausage.

SERVES 6

1. Preheat the oven to 400°F.

2. In a very large skillet over medium heat, brown the sausage, breaking it up with a wooden spoon as it cooks. Remove the sausage from the skillet to a plate and set aside.

3. Increase the heat to medium-high and melt the butter in the skillet. Add the mushrooms and sauté for 5 to 6 minutes, or until tender. Add the shallots, garlic and thyme, and sauté for about 1 minute. Add the tomatoes, paprika, fennel seeds and red pepper flakes. Bring the sauce to a boil, and then reduce the heat and simmer for 5 minutes.

4. Remove the pan from the heat and toss the sauce with the cooked ziti, the mozzarella, ½ cup of the pecorino and 2 ounces of the goat cheese.

5. Spoon the ziti and sauce into an oiled 9 x 13-inch baking dish and top with the remaining ½ cup pecorino. Spread the remaining 2 ounces goat cheese evenly over the top. Cover tightly with foil and bake for 15 minutes. Carefully remove the ziti from the oven and uncover it. Return it to the oven and bake for 10 to 15 minutes more, or until golden and bubbly. Sprinkle with parsley before serving.

1 pound wild boar link sausage, casings removed and crumbled

2 tablespoons unsalted butter

1 cup wild mushrooms

¼ cup diced shallots

2 cloves garlic, peeled and diced

2 tablespoons minced fresh thyme

One 28-ounce can chopped San Marzano tomatoes (or substitute plum tomatoes)

1 teaspoon smoked Spanish paprika

1 teaspoon fennel seeds, toasted and ground

1 teaspoon crushed red pepper flakes, or to taste

1 pound ziti, cooked al dente

1½ cups fresh mozzarella pearls (or substitute cubed fresh mozzarella)

½ cup grated pecorino cheese, plus ½ cup for garnish

2 ounces crumbled goat cheese, plus 2 ounces for garnish

2 tablespoons chopped fresh parsley, for garnish

FOR THE kiddos

Kids don't know from ziti, so I use wagon wheel pasta instead. It's fun and it has a bit more "crunch." Leave out the red pepper flakes and fennel seeds. And make prep time fun by putting out the cheese and meat ingredients and using individual casserole dishes so that the kids can build and customize their meals.

STUFFED PACCHERI
with Rapini and Ricotta

Paccheri is a big tube pasta that looks like pieces of PVC plumbing pipe. The pasta isn't especially flavorful or sophisticated. It's just that it's so darn fun. The first time Liam saw them, he started to laugh. Because of their size, they are perfect for stuffing or wearing them over each finger. The secret to this dish is limoncello. Limoncello, a lemon liqueur, is a classic Italian aperitif—that tastes great by itself. It brings a wonderful sweet-and-tart flavor to any dish. If you must, go ahead and use a different tube-shaped pasta. But go out of your way to find the limoncello. You'll be glad you did!

SERVES 4 TO 6

1. Preheat the oven to 400°F.

2. In a large skillet over medium heat, brown the sausage, breaking it up with a wooden spoon as it cooks. Add the rapini, garlic and red pepper flakes, and sauté for 5 minutes. Deglaze the pan with limoncello and cook for 2 minutes. Remove the sausage-rapini mixture from the heat and set aside.

3. In a medium bowl, whisk the egg and then stir in the ricotta, Parmigiano-Reggiano, lemon juice and zest, scallions and parsley. Fold the cheese mixture into the sausage-rapini mixture in the skillet and mix well.

4. Spread 1 cup of the sauce on the bottom of a 9 x 13-inch baking dish. Fill a piping bag fitted with a standard tip (or use a resealable plastic sandwich bag with a corner cut off) with the sausage-cheese filling and fill each paccheri. Carefully place each filled paccheri in the baking dish.

5. Spoon the remaining 1 cup sauce over the paccheri, cover tightly with aluminum foil and bake for 15 minutes. Uncover and then bake for 15 minutes more, or until bubbly. Remove the paccheri from the oven and let stand for 5 minutes. Garnish with the basil leaves before serving.

2 spicy fennel link sausages (approximately 1/2 pound), casings removed and diced

1 cup minced broccoli rabe or straight up broccoli

4 cloves garlic, peeled and minced

1 to 2 teaspoons crushed red pepper flakes, or to taste

1/4 cup limoncello (or substitute white wine mixed with the juice and zest of a lemon)

1 large egg

One 16-ounce container whole-milk Italian ricotta, drained

1/2 cup grated Parmigiano-Reggiano cheese

Juice and zest of 1 small lemon

1 scallion, root end removed and minced

1 tablespoon chopped fresh parsley

2 cups Quick Tomato Sauce, or more if desired (page 132)

3/4 pound paccheri pasta, cooked al dente

8 fresh basil leaves, for garnish

FOR THE kiddos

You're going to see some smiles among your junior crew when you serve this one up. Giant tube pasta just has a way of tickling the funny bone. The kids like to eat the filling first and then use the tubes as telescopes. Just remember, go easy on the garlic and red pepper flakes, but otherwise, this

BUTTERNUT SQUASH GNOCCHI
with Sage and Mushroom Brown Butter

Chefs love gnocchi for its ability to sponge up flavors like, well, a sponge. I decided to take that idea one step further and mix in extra flavor by blending rich, sweet butternut squash with the potatoes for the gnocchi dough. Throw in some sage and browned butter, and you have a mess of delicate flavors that are just about irresistible. The gnocchi aren't hard to make, but you really have to use a kitchen tool called a ricer if you want to avoid gummy, chewy gnocchi. You can mash the potatoes with the squash, but I suggest you buy or borrow a ricer. You'll be glad you did.

SERVES 4 TO 6

1. Preheat the oven to 425°F. Line a baking sheet with parchment paper. Lightly flour the parchment paper.

2. Season the squash with ½ teaspoon each of the salt and pepper. Drizzle oil over each half, top with butter, and then spread the sage, thyme and garlic cloves evenly over each half. Roast the squash until tender, 1 to 1½ hours.

3. While the squash is roasting, boil the potato until tender. Keep warm. Once the squash is cool enough to handle, scoop the flesh out of the skin. Run the still-warm potato and the squash through a potato ricer into a medium bowl.

4. In a small bowl, whisk together the ricotta, 2 tablespoons of the Parmesan, egg, nutmeg, the remaining ½ teaspoon salt and remaining ¼ teaspoon pepper.

5. Sprinkle a work surface with ½ cup of the flour and make a mound of the squash-potato mixture in the center of it. Create a well in the middle of the mound and spoon the ricotta mixture into it. Sprinkle generously with 1 cup of the flour. Mix everything together until just incorporated. Add the remaining ½ cup flour, a little at a time, and only as much as necessary, and knead until the dough just holds together and is barely sticking to your fingers. (Don't overwork the dough.)

6. Cut the dough into 8 even pieces. Working with 1 piece at a time, roll it on a lightly floured surface into a 1-inch-thick rope, and cut the rope into 1-inch pieces. Continue until you've rolled all the dough

continued on next page >>>

Gnocchi

Flour, for dusting the baking sheet

One 1-pound butternut squash, cut in half lengthwise and seeds removed

1 teaspoons salt, divided

¾ teaspoon pepper, divided

2 tablespoons olive oil

4 tablespoons unsalted butter

4 sprigs fresh sage

4 sprigs fresh thyme

1 head garlic, halved

1 medium russet potato

¾ cup ricotta cheese

2 tablespoons grated Parmesan cheese, plus 6 tablespoons

1 large egg, beaten

2 teaspoons ground nutmeg

2 cups all-purpose flour, divided, plus more for dusting

Sauce

8 tablespoons unsalted butter, divided

1 cup sliced fresh porcini mushrooms (or substitute shiitake)

Salt and freshly ground black pepper, to taste

2 tablespoons minced shallots

1 tablespoon minced garlic

13 fresh sage leaves

2 tablespoons freshly squeezed lemon juice

¼ cup mascarpone cheese

Zest of 1 large lemon

pieces and cut all the gnocchi. Arrange the gnocchi on the prepared baking sheet.

7. Bring a large pot of water to a boil over medium-high heat, and salt it generously. Meanwhile, prepare the sauce. Melt 2 tablespoons of the butter in a large saucepan over medium heat, and sauté the mushrooms until they have browned, about 5 minutes. Season with salt and pepper.

8. Add the shallots and garlic, and cook until tender, about 4 minutes. Add the remaining 6 tablespoons butter, and then swirl the saucepan and scrape up the brown bits on the bottom with a wooden spoon. Stir in the sage. When the butter is brown and has a nutty aroma, remove the saucepan from the heat. Stir in the lemon juice.

9. Cook the gnocchi in the boiling water, working in batches, until they float to the surface, 1 to 2 minutes. Then scoop them out with a slotted spoon and carefully add them to the saucepan of sauce. When you've added all the gnocchi to the sauce, add the mascarpone and lemon zest, and toss gently to combine. (The mascarpone may curdle because of the lemon juice, but this won't affect the taste.) Serve at once.

FOR THE **kiddos**

My kids love gnocchi, as do most of their friends. The gnocchi are bite-size and look fun on the plate. (I sometimes spell out names or make letters or shapes out of them.) I don't, however, mention that the gnocchi are made with squash. I like to avoid any potential "ewww." I figure a little white lie, like "They're potato balls," is worth it if you can get youngsters to clean their plates. Also, eliminate the mushrooms from the sauce if that's a deal breaker for your little ones, or at the very least, dice the mushrooms up fine.

BRAISED PORK BELLY RAVIOLI
with Roasted Plum Tomato Sauce

Braising is one of my favorite ways to cook because it saturates whatever you're cooking with flavor and makes meat fall-apart tender. It's the perfect way to cook meat for ravioli filling, and I use the most flavorful cuts of pork for this special-occasion recipe. This one takes a bit of prep work. You can braise the meat a few days ahead of time, and you can even make the ravioli at your convenience and freeze them for up to three months. In any case, I would love to see somebody try to frown after eating ravioli. Impossible.

SERVES 4 TO 6

1. Preheat the oven to 300°F.

2. Season the pork belly and pork cheeks liberally with 2 tablespoons of each salt and pepper. Let sit for 10 to 15 minutes.

3. Heat 2 tablespoons of the oil in a large cast-iron skillet or other heavy skillet over medium-high heat. Add the pork belly and cook for 3 to 4 minutes per side, or until browned. Transfer the browned pork belly to a roasting pan. Cook the pork cheeks in the same manner and add them to the roasting pan.

4. Toast the cumin seeds, fennel seeds, cinnamon stick and peppercorns in the skillet over medium heat until fragrant, about 2 minutes. Add the chicken stock and 3 cloves of the garlic, and bring to a boil. Pour this over the pork in the roasting pan and top with the sprigs of thyme and the bay leaf. Cover the roasting pan with a lid or with aluminum foil (fitting it as snugly as possible). Braise the pork in the oven until fork-tender, about 2 to 2½ hours.

5. While the pork is braising, prepare the sauce. Place the tomatoes, cut side up, in a baking dish and season with salt and pepper. Scatter the remaining 5 cloves of garlic over the tomatoes. Top with 2 tablespoons of the oil and the sprigs of oregano.

6. Roast the tomatoes in the oven (while the pork is braising) for 40 to 50 minutes, or until soft and lightly browned. Remove the tomatoes from the oven and let them cool to room temperature. Coarsely chop the tomatoes, and discard the oregano sprigs. Dice the garlic.

7. Heat the remaining 1 tablespoon oil in a large skillet over medium-high heat, and sauté the shallots until tender and caramelized.

1 pound pork belly, skin on

¾ pound pork cheeks, cut into 2-inch pieces (or substitute pork shoulder)

2 tablespoons salt, plus more for seasoning

2 tablespoons freshly cracked black pepper, plus more for seasoning

5 tablespoons olive oil, divided

2 teaspoons cumin seeds

1 teaspoon fennel seeds

1 cinnamon stick

8 black peppercorns

6 cups chicken stock

3 cloves garlic (peel on), plus 5 cloves, peeled and smashed

3 sprigs fresh thyme

1 fresh bay leaf

1½ pounds plum tomatoes, halved

5 sprigs fresh oregano

2 shallots, peeled and chopped

1 cup white wine (preferably Pinot Grigio)

3 tablespoons unsalted butter

1¼ cups ricotta cheese

½ cup grated Parmigiano-Reggiano cheese, plus ¼ cup for garnish

1½ pounds pasta dough (see my homemade pasta dough recipe on my website)

1 large egg beaten with 1 tablespoon water (egg wash)

Crispy Prosciutto (page 150; optional)

continued on next page ›››

Add the diced garlic and deglaze the pan with the white wine. Reduce the liquid by half. Add the tomatoes and simmer for about 30 minutes, stirring often. Gradually stir in the butter to finish the sauce.

8. Prepare the ravioli filling. Shred the pork cheek. Remove the pork belly skin and dice the pork belly into ¼-inch lardons.

9. In a large bowl, combine the shredded pork cheek, the ricotta and ½ cup of the Parmigiano-Reggiano, and mix until combined. Fold in the pork belly. Refrigerate the filling until you're ready to assemble the ravioli.

10. Cut circles out of the sheets of pasta dough with a 3-inch biscuit cutter. Place 1 tablespoon of the pork filling slightly off center on a dough circle. Brush the edges of the circle with egg wash and then fold in half, being careful to press out the excess air. Crimp the edges closed with the tines of a fork.

11. Cook the ravioli in batches. Fill a large pot three-quarters full with water and salt it heavily. Bring the water to a boil over high heat, reduce the heat to medium and add some of the ravioli. Cook the ravioli for about 3 minutes. Scoop them out with a slotted spoon and carefully add them to the tomato sauce. Cook the remaining batches in the same way.

12. Serve the ravioli garnished with the remaining ¼ cup Parmigiano-Reggiano and the Crispy Prosciutto, if desired.

Dean's Food 411
CRISPY PROSCIUTTO

How about a crackling good garnish for your pasta (or salads or eggs or …)? I love making my own Crispy Prosciutto to top off my homemade ravioli or just about any pasta dish, and if you seal it up tight in a container, it will be usable for a week or more. You can use this treat just about anywhere crumbled bacon would go, and the kids absolutely love it. Not to mention, it's super easy and quick to whip up.

Preheat the oven to 375°F and line a baking sheet with parchment paper. Lay 8 slices of prosciutto on the baking sheet and bake until crispy, 12 to 15 minutes. (Don't overcook them—they'll cook a little more as they cool.) Remove and let cool before breaking the slices up into smaller bits.

FOR THE kiddos

Kids go bonkers for ravioli, and the roasted tomato sauce I use with these homemade beauties works just as well for the young ones as it does for adults. Make this a fun, memorable meal for the little ones by letting them use special cookie cutters to cut out the ravioli dough. Try dinosaurs, letters or other interesting shapes. Kids love to "glop" the filling in the ravioli, and they also enjoy learning how to crimp the edges so that the filling doesn't escape. It's also a good idea to dial back the flavors just a bit; you might want to leave out the fennel and cumin. And keep the words *cheek* and *belly* to yourself.

Super-cheesy, Super-easy
MUSHROOM RISOTTO

Properly cooked, a risotto is a velvety treat, one that is the perfect platform for just about any savory flavor, but especially cheese. The key to making a risotto that is all it can be is to slowly introduce stock to the rice so that the rice gradually absorbs the liquid and releases its starch—making for a silky smooth texture. That's the sign you've got it right. (You'll know you don't if you wind up with a gummy, sticky rice mixture.) Stirring is also key, and the best risotto requires constant stirring, which is kind of meditative. I've added three different cheeses to make the flavors a little more complex and the texture just a little creamier.

SERVES 6 TO 8

1. Heat the stock in a large pot over medium heat.

2. Heat the oil in another large pot over medium heat, and sauté the onions until translucent. Add the mushrooms and garlic, and sauté until slightly browned, about 5 minutes.

3. Add the rice to the pot with the vegetables and cook, stirring, for 2 minutes. Do not brown the rice. Stir in the scallions and thyme, and add the wine. Cook until the liquid is almost evaporated.

4. Add warm stock one ladle at a time to the rice, stirring constantly. Allow the stock to be completely absorbed before adding the next ladleful. This step takes patience, so don't rush. Cook the rice until it's al dente, about 20 minutes. Add the salt, pepper and butter.

5. Reserve a couple of tablespoons of the parsley for garnish. Add the three cheeses and stir to combine. Add the lemon juice and the zest, and the chopped parsley. Garnish with the ¼ cup of each Parmesean and Romano and the reserved parsley. Serve hot.

8 to 10 cups vegetable stock

2 tablespoons olive oil

½ cup diced yellow onion

¾ pound mushrooms, sliced (a mix of button and wild mushrooms)

3 cloves garlic, peeled and minced

1 pound arborio rice

2 scallions, root ends removed and minced

2 tablespoons minced fresh thyme

⅔ cup dry white wine

Salt and freshly cracked black pepper, to taste

4 tablespoons unsalted butter

½ cup cubed fontina cheese

¼ cup grated Parmesan cheese, plus ¼ cup for garnish

¼ cup grated Romano cheese, plus ¼ cup for garnish

Juice and zest of 1 lemon

¼ cup chopped fresh parsley

As much as I love the silky smooth texture of risotto, kids tend to find it uninteresting and, well, mushy looking (Liam's words, not mine). So I use the same recipe for the adult version, but I fry up some "rice balls" for the kids. Finely dice the mushrooms, and when adding the cheeses in the final cooking step, swap the fontina for fresh mozzarella. However, instead of stirring the mozzarella into the rice, put a cube of mozzarella in the middle of each rice ball, for a gooey center that will surprise and delight the little guys. Use a small ice-cream scoop to make 2-inch balls out of the risotto mixture. Set up a breading station and toss each ball in flour, egg wash (an egg whisked with 1 teaspoon water), and panko bread crumbs seasoned with a tablespoon or two of Parmesan. Heat 1 inch of canola oil in a large deep saucepan over medium heat until the temperature reaches 350°F. Fry the balls in batches until golden brown, let them cool slightly and serve with a side of Quick Tomato Sauce (page 132).

DEANO'S PRIMAVERA
à la Tons of Garlic

I didn't grow up around a lot of vegetables. Well, not a lot of fresh vegetables. There was the occasional boiled-to-death spinach or mushy frozen peas, but salads weren't big in my house. It wasn't until my early twenties, when I was working at a restaurant called Lime Rickey's Diner, that I discovered how wonderful a medley of fresh vegetables can be. They had an incredible pasta primavera that I ate almost every day. So when I decided to create my own version, I wanted to capture the fresh, brilliant flavor and stunning colors in that dish. I use it to top off a wealth of seasonal vegetables with a strong dose of garlic, two types of tomatoes and a handful of goat cheese. But as much as I love this recipe, there is a lot of room for adaptation. Sub in your favorite pasta, in-season vegetables, different cheese (or no cheese at all) and your favorite dressing. Just cut all the vegetables the same size to avoid that sin of sins: soggy, overcooked vegetables mixed with undercooked vegetables.

SERVES 4 TO 6

1. Heat the oil in a large saucepan over medium heat, and sauté the shallots until tender. Add the garlic and sauté for 1 minute, stirring constantly.

2. Add the zucchini, yellow squash, bell pepper, broccoli, asparagus, thyme and red pepper flakes. Stir-fry until the vegetables are tender-crisp, about 7 minutes. Taste and season with salt and pepper.

3. Add the cherry tomatoes and the sun-dried tomatoes and cook for 1 minute, or until the cherry tomatoes start to soften. Add the cooked rotini and then transfer the primavera to a serving bowl.

4. Gently toss with the pine nuts, goat cheese and the slivered basil. Serve the primavera warm so that the goat cheese is slightly melted. Garnish each serving with a whole basil leaf.

2 tablespoons olive oil

2 tablespoons minced shallots

2 cloves garlic, peeled and minced

2 medium zucchini, ends trimmed and diced

1 medium yellow crookneck squash, ends trimmed and diced

1 red bell pepper, seeded and diced

1 cup broccoli florets

4 asparagus spears, ends trimmed and cut into 1-inch pieces

2 tablespoons fresh thyme

1 to 2 teaspoons crushed red pepper flakes, or to taste

Salt and freshly ground black pepper, to taste

½ cup halved cherry tomatoes

¼ cup sliced sun-dried tomatoes

1 pound rotini, cooked al dente

¼ cup toasted pine nuts

½ cup crumbled goat cheese

¼ cup slivered fresh basil leaves, plus 6 whole leaves for garnish

FOR THE kiddos

Although this is a Stella's Choice recipe, I pull back on the spices a bit and use my kids' favorite pasta, elbow macaroni. You know your kids best, so for maximum success, use vegetables that they really like. But don't panic if there's a side dish worth of veggies left over after they're done eating. We'll get there!

LINGUINI AGLIO E OLIO WITH TUNA
and Red Pepper Flakes

STELLA'S CHOICE

Traditionally, aglio e olio (Italian for "garlic and oil") is made with spaghetti and little else but the title ingredients. I give it an update with a little more oomph by adding some freshly grilled tuna and spices. At the heart of the dish is a hot infused oil mix that intensifies the garlic and chili flavors and can be used in lots of other dishes, on top of your favorite pasta or even on eggs.

SERVES 4

1. Heat the olive oil in a small pot over medium heat, and sauté the garlic briefly, just until the oil starts to bubble and simmer. Remove the pot from the heat and add the red pepper flakes. Cover and let cool. Then strain the oil, discarding the garlic and red pepper flakes. Set the garlic oil aside.

2. In a small bowl, mix the coriander, chili powder and cumin. Spread the spice rub evenly over a large plate. Roll the ahi tuna in it, pressing down to ensure the spices stick to the tuna. Season the tuna with salt and pepper, and set aside.

3. Heat a medium cast-iron skillet over high heat. Add the canola oil and reduce the heat to medium-high. Sear the ahi tuna until golden on all sides, 1½ minutes per side. Be careful not to burn the spice coating or overcook the tuna.

4. Remove the tuna to a paper towel–lined plate and cut it into ½-inch slices. Set aside 4 slices and cut the remaining slices into bite-size pieces.

5. In a large bowl, combine the warm linguini with the lemon juice, lemon zest, 1 tablespoon of the parsley, the parsley leaves, 2 tablespoons of the pecorino and enough of the reserved garlic oil to coat. Toss to combine well. Fold in the bite-size tuna pieces.

6. Arrange the pasta on each of 4 plates and garnish with the reserved tuna slices, the remaining 1 tablespoon parsley and the remaining 2 tablespoons pecorino. Serve at once.

½ cup extra-virgin olive oil

3 cloves garlic, peeled and sliced

1 tablespoon crushed red pepper flakes

1 teaspoon ground coriander

½ teaspoon chili powder

½ teaspoon ground cumin

½ pound fresh ahi tuna loin

Salt and freshly ground black pepper, to taste

1 tablespoon canola oil

1 pound fresh linguini, cooked al dente

2 tablespoons freshly squeezed lemon juice

Zest of 1 lemon

1 tablespoon chopped fresh parsley, plus 1 tablespoon for garnish

¼ cup fresh parsley leaves

2 tablespoons grated pecorino cheese, plus 2 tablespoons for garnish

Chapter seven

A LITTLE ON THE SIDE

Yes, I yam a porcupine fry

As a father of five kids and a guy staring down the other side of his forties, I can finally and proudly say, "There isn't a vegetable out there I don't like." This is no small feat. For all of my childhood and most of my adult years, I thought "a side" was boiled potatoes, mashed potatoes, baked potatoes or French fries. On fancy occasions like Thanksgiving, we would occasionally have scalloped potatoes.

Any other "sides" we had were straight out of a can or cooked-to-death vegetables. Actually, I wouldn't exactly call them sides. More like cruel and unusual punishment. I had other names for them as well: "Blech," "Eww," "What the...?" and "Oh, good God, no."

I remember the first time I took a leap of faith and tried brussels sprouts in a restaurant. They were blanched, then sautéed with garlic and bacon. I think my hand was shaking as I brought a forkful of this evil vegetable up to my mouth. Then the unthinkable happened. My taste buds were dazzled by the tang of vinegar, followed by smooth, salty bacon and backed up with a delicate, pleasing crunch. Wait a minute. Brussels sprouts don't crunch! They go *plflllt*. Was it an accident? Did the chef undercook them? Who puts bacon and vinegar on brussels sprouts? I began to realize that this wasn't a mistake, but how brussels sprouts were meant to be cooked. I realized that it was actually how most vegetables should be cooked. Blanched first and finished off in a sauté pan with seasonings, butter and fresh herbs. What could be better?

Knowing that veggies and potatoes were no longer a punishment for a crime I didn't commit, they suddenly became a wonderful way to add flavor and diversity to the main course. And the possibilities were suddenly awe inspiring. The variety of vegetables, tubers, roots and grains spread out before me was endless. I knew then that the sky truly is the limit when it comes to delectable side dishes.

I've captured that diversity in the recipes that follow. You'll find incredibly tasty and healthy ways to prepare sides of all types, from potatoes to vegetables to leafy greens. I've also thrown in some advice on sneaking these misunderstood ingredients into great recipes that will have your kids eating onions, broccoli and cauliflower. They might even ask for seconds. And don't worry about having to spend the better part of your evening in the kitchen; I've made sure that these recipes are just about as easy as opening a can. No more overcooked veggies and lumpy potatoes!

Liam's Favorite
DUCHESS POTATOES

I have nothing against plain old mashed potatoes. (I've certainly eaten my fill—especially the lumpy, bland variety.) But if you're going to go with this standard, why not dress it up a little bit and have some fun with your potatoes? Duchess potatoes are perfect for kids, who can finish one in two bites. I've kept my version tame and simple for two reasons—the basic flavors go perfectly with any main course (so no complaints from even the most finicky eater) and, more importantly, you can whip up these delightful mounds in no time at all.

SERVES 4

1. Preheat the oven to 450°F. Line a baking sheet with parchment paper.

2. In a medium pot, cover the potatoes with cold water and place over medium-high heat. Bring to a boil and salt heavily, until the water tastes like the ocean. Reduce the heat and simmer until the potatoes are fork-tender, 18 to 20 minutes.

3. Strain the potatoes in a colander. When they are cool enough to handle, pass them through a potato ricer, or mash them by hand with a hand masher.

4. Return the potatoes to the pot and add the egg yolks, butter, salt, pepper and nutmeg. Cook over medium heat, stirring frequently with a wooden spoon, until the potato mixture comes away from the sides of the pot, 1 to 2 minutes. The consistency should be slightly sticky, yet firm.

5. Let the potato mixture cool and then fill a piping bag fitted with a star tip. Pipe 2-inch mounds on the prepared baking sheet. (If you don't have a piping bag you can use a resealable freezer bag with a corner cut off, or even a spoon, to create the mounds.)

6. Sprinkle the Parmesan over the top of the mounds and then bake until golden brown, about 15 minutes.

2 large russet potatoes, peeled and quartered

2 large egg yolks

4 tablespoons unsalted butter

1 teaspoon salt

1 teaspoon freshly cracked black pepper

Pinch of ground nutmeg

1/2 cup finely grated Parmesan cheese

FOR THE kiddos

This is an awesome side dish for kids, with ingredients every kid will love. But you can make it even more appealing by getting kids involved with the piping process. Little ones get a huge kick out of piping anything, because it's like fooling around with Play-Doh. Let them choose funky tips and make whatever shapes they want (as long as the size of the potato mounds are roughly the same so that they'll cook evenly). Want to go a little bit more wild? Color those taters! Divide the potato mixture up into small batches and let the kids add a different food coloring to each batch. Then they can pipe out their own little rainbow side dish.

GRILLED GREEN BEANS
with Parmesan and Pine Nuts

Having grown up in Canada, I appreciate living in Southern California more than you can imagine. Tori and I do a lot of our cooking, living and parenting in the backyard, because L.A. has two seasons: summer and cooler summer. You'll find the whole family hanging out around the grill at least a couple of nights a week, and I prefer to cook the whole meal on the grill if possible. I also like things simple, quick, fresh and flavorful, and this scrumptious side dish achieves all four. Grilling brings out the simple, almost nutty flavor of the beans and is the best way to prepare green beans in my mind. Just add a little Parm, some toasted pine nuts and a touch of lemon, and you're good to go. No need to change it up for the kiddos. They'll wolf it down just as it is. (The adults may even have to fight for their share!)

1 **pound fresh green beans,** cleaned and ends trimmed

2 **tablespoons olive oil**

Salt and black pepper, to taste

Zest of 1 lemon

¼ **cup freshly grated** Parmesan cheese

¼ **cup toasted pine nuts**

SERVES 4 TO 6

1. Fill a large bowl with 1 part ice and 3 parts water. Fill a large pot with heavily salted water and bring to a boil over high heat. Plunge the green beans into the boiling water and cook just until they turn bright green, about 2 minutes. Quickly transfer them to the ice bath. Once they have chilled, remove the green beans to a paper towel–lined plate and pat dry.

2. Place the green beans in a medium bowl, add the oil and toss to coat. Season with salt and pepper.

3. Preheat a grill to medium. Using a greased grill basket, grill the green beans. (A greased grill basket will make grilling the green beans much easier.) Turn them frequently until they're tender and brown in spots, 8 to 10 minutes.

4. Remove the green beans to a serving dish and toss with the lemon zest. Sprinkle with the Parmesan and pine nuts before serving.

McDERMOTT PORCUPINE FRIES

You'll want to get the kids in the kitchen for this one, because the last part of the cooking process is like a magic trick. You do a little fancy cutting (don't worry, it's not hard) and wait for a wonderful effect that's about a hundred times better than your basic French fries. And as much as kids flip to watch each porcupine "bloom," they really love to eat these things up. My kids actually ask for them on a regular basis, and I'm always up for making them. Plus, they go perfectly with main dishes fancy or plain. You can mix it up a little bit by using different types of potatoes. Think purple potato porcupine fries. Say that five times fast.

2 large russet potatoes

¼ to ½ cup canola oil

Salt and freshly cracked pepper, to taste

SERVES 2 TO 4

1. Preheat the oven to 400°F.

2. Cut each potato in half lengthwise. Place a potato half cut side down on a flat surface. Slice across the width of the potato half every ¼ inch or so, being careful not to cut all the way through. Lay the shaft of a wooden spoon alongside the potato and perpendicular to your knife as a stop guide. Then cut lengthwise every ¼ inch or so, transforming the semicircles you just cut into the "quills" of the porcupine. Again, don't cut all the way through the potato. (The wooden spoon really helps with this process.) Repeat this process for the remaining potato halves.

3. Space the potato halves evenly apart on a nonstick baking sheet, cut side down. Drizzle each with the oil and season with salt and pepper. Bake until tender and golden brown and until the "porcupine quills" have bloomed, about 40 minutes. Serve and watch the smiles begin.

RAINBOW CHARD
with Bacon and Capers

Chard, like spinach and other earthy greens, is chock-full of nutrients that kids and adults need. In raw form, chard is an acquired taste (that's a nice way of saying kids will spit it out). But braise or sauté these greens and they come to life. Any leafy greens like this need to be thoroughly rinsed before cooking—otherwise you risk a gritty mouth feel. For young chard, trim just the stems; for mature chard, discard the spines then chop and cook the stems. If larger, more mature chard leaves are all that are available, they are going to be more bitter than young chard. You might want to add about a teaspoon of sugar or agave nectar to the dish to mellow any bitterness and bring out the sweetness in the greens. For the kids, I chop the chard fine, leave out the cayenne and double the bacon.

2 bunches rainbow chard

3 slices thick-cut bacon, cut in 1-inch cubes (for lardons)

2 cloves garlic, peeled and smashed

1 shallot, peeled and thinly sliced

1 teaspoon black pepper

½ teaspoon salt

¼ teaspoon cayenne pepper

¼ cup capers, drained

Zest of 1 lemon

SERVES 4

1. Separate the chard leaves from the stems. Wash, rinse and dry the leaves and stems thoroughly. Slice the leaves lengthwise into ribbons, and slice the stems crosswise into ½-inch pieces. Set aside.

2. Cook the bacon in a large cast-iron skillet over medium heat until it is crispy, turning occasionally. Transfer the lardons to a paper towel–lined plate and set aside.

3. Add the chard stems, garlic and shallots to the skillet, and cook for 3 to 5 minutes. Remove the garlic and discard.

4. Increase the heat to medium-high, add the chard leaves and toss with tongs until just wilted, 1 to 2 minutes. Season with the black pepper, salt and cayenne pepper. Stir in the reserved lardons, the capers and the lemon zest, and toss to combine. Serve hot.

BAKED CAULIFLOWER
in a Curry Cheese Sauce

Cauliflower's "Plain Jane" persona makes it a perfect flavor sponge for a rich and savory sauce like this, and curry is an ideal pairing. I got this idea from a friend who used to make something similar, but I've dressed my version up with three different cheeses that give it a little more complexity and fun. You can also steam or pan roast the cauliflower, but no matter how you cook it, it's one healthy vegetable with one delicious sauce.

SERVES 4

1. Preheat the oven to 400°F.

2. In a large pot filled with salted water over high heat, boil the cauliflower just until tender, 6 to 7 minutes. Drain the cauliflower, transfer it to a ceramic casserole dish and set aside.

3. Melt the butter in a medium saucepan over medium heat. Whisk in the flour and curry to form a paste and cook, stirring frequently, for 2 minutes. Slowly whisk in the milk to ensure a smooth consistency.

4. Bring the sauce to a boil, stirring constantly, and then reduce the heat to a simmer. Whisk in the cheddar cheese, the goat cheese and the Parmigiano-Reggiano cheese and cook until fully incorporated. Taste and season with salt and pepper.

5. Pour the sauce over the cauliflower and bake until bubbly and light golden brown, about 15 minutes.

6. Carefully transfer the cauliflower to a serving platter and pour any sauce that remains in the casserole dish over it. Sprinkle paprika over the cauliflower and serve at once.

1 head cauliflower, cored and cut into florets

2 tablespoons unsalted butter

2 tablespoons all-purpose flour

1 tablespoon curry powder

½ cup cold whole milk

¼ cup grated sharp cheddar cheese

¼ cup crumbled goat cheese

2 tablespoons finely grated Parmigiano-Reggiano cheese

Salt and freshly cracked black pepper, to taste

1½ teaspoons paprika

FOR THE **kiddos**

Cut a few bite-size florets off the head of cauliflower and bake or steam them until tender. Then put them in individual ramekins or little casserole dishes. Whip up the sauce with only a pinch of curry, and cover the florets with the sauce. Bake in a 375°F oven until the top is golden brown, remove and let cool, and serve with the kids' favorite main course. You can also tell the kids they're yellow, cheesy veggie brains. Don't ask; it works.

POTATO BUG POUTINE

This easy side dish is a nod to my Canadian roots. The "bugs" look great on the plate, are fun to make with kids and are amazingly tasty. These potatoes are a true, all-purpose side that will go with just about any main dish. I love this so much, I'd serve it with a peanut butter sandwich. Seriously.

SERVES 6

1. Melt the butter in a saucepan over medium heat, and add the flour. Cook, stirring, until the mixture is smooth, about 2 minutes.

2. Add the beef stock, ketchup and vinegar, and bring to a boil. Continue to stir until the sauce thickens, about 6 minutes. Remove from the heat, and taste and season with salt and pepper. Set the sauce aside and keep warm.

3. Prepare the "bugs." Cut each sweet potato in half lengthwise. Set a sweet potato half on a cutting board, cut-side down, and cut thin slices across it—without cutting all the way through—to create an accordion fan. Repeat this process with the remaining sweet potato halves.

4. Add the oil to a large high-sided frying pan or a deep fryer (add more oil, if needed, to cover the potatoes). Heat the oil over high heat until it reaches 350°F.

5. Use tongs to place the sweet potatoes in the oil. Fry the sweet potatoes in batches if necessary to avoid overcrowding. Cook until crispy on the outside and tender on the inside. Remove the sweet potatoes to a paper towel–lined plate to drain the excess oil.

6. With the tip of a sharp knife, poke two little holes at one end of each "bug," and stick a chive in each hole for antennae. Dust the sweet potatoes with salt and pepper, top with the cheese curds and then cover with the reserved poutine gravy. Serve hot.

Poutine Gravy

4 tablespoons unsalted butter

¼ cup flour

4 cups beef stock

2 tablespoons ketchup

1 tablespoon cider vinegar

Salt and black pepper, to taste

Bugs

6 small sweet potatoes

2 cups canola oil (depending on the size of pan)

1 bunch fresh chives

Salt and black pepper, to taste

1 cup cheese curds

MINTED PEAS, LIMA BEANS AND BACON

If you grew up like I did, pre–Food Network, you probably also had an early revulsion to peas. That's because they came in one form: a mushy near-gruel. Those weren't peas; they were punishment. Time to rethink peas. Minted peas are a much beloved regular addition to British dinners. I'm careful to keep my peas super crisp with just a quick blanch (one of the best methods ever for cooking vegetables without losing their natural freshness and texture). Substitute pancetta or even Crispy Prosciutto (page 150) for the bacon in this recipe, but personally, I like the heartiness the bacon brings to a dish full of bright and sparkly flavors. Pip, pip, cheerio and the like.

¾ **pound fresh peas**

¾ **pound fresh lima beans**

6 **slices slab bacon**

1 **bunch fresh mint, stems removed**

Salt and black pepper, to taste

Juice and zest of 1 small lime

SERVES 4 TO 6

1. Fill a large bowl nearly full with 1 part ice and 3 parts water and set a colander inside.

2. Bring a large pot of heavily salted water to a boil. Using a slotted spoon, immerse the peas in the boiling water for about 1 minute, or until vibrant green. Remove them to the colander in the ice bath. Repeat the process with the lima beans, refreshing the ice bath if necessary.

3. In a large cast-iron skillet over medium heat, render the bacon strips until crispy, reserving the fat. Remove the bacon to a plate, pat it dry with paper towels and crumble it. Set the bacon aside.

4. Cut about three-quarters of the mint into slivers. Set aside.

5. Leave enough bacon fat in the skillet just to coat, and sauté the peas and lima beans for 1 minute. Stir in the reserved bacon and the slivered mint, and then season with salt and pepper.

6. Serve on a platter family style and garnish with the whole mint leaves, the lime juice and the lime zest.

FOR THE **kiddos**

Get the kids shucking peas, and they'll be having fun without knowing it's work. It also gets them familiar with the wonderful raw nature of peas, so they will be more open to the blanched version. I love to teach my kids how vegetables look, taste and smell raw and cooked, as fuel for their imaginations. Serve adults and kids from the same platter for this dish.

If the fresh green beans on offer at your local market are a little bit large, you might consider using haricot vert or another smaller, thinner green bean variety for the kids. They find smaller beans more manageable and more enticing. When making this dish for the youngsters, I prepare the green beans and wrap and bake them just as I would with the adult version, but I do without the sauce. Instead, top the green beans with just a little butter and salt and pepper. Add a squeeze of fresh lemon juice just before serving.

Tori's
GREEN BEAN BUNDLES

STELLA'S CHOICE

This is a Tori classic. My wife loves eating them, so I love making them. We like to include them in special-occasion meals, because they look like little presents when you serve them. The flavors are all about the savory—the clean, fresh snap and light taste of the green beans contrast the richness of the bacon and the saltiness of the sauce. This dish is also ripe for a little creative experimentation. Add a tiny bit of minced ginger to the sauce, or even a dose of chopped garlic, to complicate the mix of flavors. Some people even like to add a bit of brown sugar for a sweet-and-savory vibe. But no matter how you might change it up, I'd suggest making the most of the presentation—these delicious delights deserve a fancy serving platter.

2 pounds green beans, ends trimmed

8 slices slab bacon

2 tablespoons soy sauce

3 tablespoons oyster sauce

2 tablespoons unsalted butter, melted

Salt and black pepper, to taste

SERVES 4 TO 6

1. Preheat the oven to 350°F.

2. Fill a large bowl half full with 1 part ice and 3 parts water.

3. Bring a large pot of heavily salted water to a boil. Plunge the green beans into the boiling water and cook just until they turn bright green, about 2 minutes. Quickly remove them with a mesh strainer to the ice bath. When the green beans have chilled, transfer them to a clean kitchen towel to dry. Set aside.

4. In a large cast-iron skillet over medium heat, cook the bacon just until it starts to brown, about 2 minutes per side. (It should not be crisp.) Remove the bacon to a paper towel–lined plate, pat dry and set aside to cool.

5. Whisk together the soy sauce, oyster sauce and butter in a small bowl.

6. Once the bacon is cool, cut each bacon strip in half lengthwise. Arrange the bacon strips on a clean work surface so that they are parallel. Divide the green beans evenly among the bacon strips, and wrap the bacon around the green beans to hold them together.

7. Place each green bean bundle in a large baking dish, with the seam where the bacon ends meet facing down. Drizzle with half of the sauce. Season lightly with salt and pepper. Bake until the bacon is crispy, 20 to 30 minutes. Give the remaining sauce a quick stir, pour it over the bundles and serve at once.

Creamy, Cheesy
CORN AND PANCETTA

When you have a pack of kids to feed (homework to find, diapers to change, fights to referee, scratched knees to kiss and make better, etc.), there are times when only comfort food will do. When one of those nights rolls around and I'm looking to get a relaxed, informal dinner on the table, I go for something like this velvety, super-filling side. It eats like a main course and has the irresistible allure of mac and cheese with the garden goodness of fresh corn. That's because of my homemade creamed corn. You can certainly substitute canned creamed corn, but I'd recommend you go fresh, if possible. You will really taste the difference. Don't be surprised if the main course loses out to seconds of this side dish. For the kids, you might want to cut out the parsley and chives. Otherwise, they'll eat it up as is!

SERVES 4 TO 6

2 tablespoons unsalted butter

1 red onion, peeled and finely diced

6 ears corn, husked, rinsed, and kernels cut off the cob

2 tablespoons fresh thyme

Salt and freshly cracked black pepper, to taste

½ cup heavy cream

½ cup thinly sliced pancetta

One 4-ounce log goat cheese, crumbled

1 cup finely grated sharp cheddar cheese

2 tablespoons chopped fresh parsley, for garnish

1 tablespoon chopped fresh chives, for garnish

1. Melt the butter in a large pot over medium-high heat, and sauté the red onions until tender, about 4 minutes. Add the corn and thyme, and sauté for 3 minutes, stirring frequently. Season with salt and pepper.

2. Cover with ¼ cup water and bring the corn mixture to a boil. Reduce the heat and simmer until the corn is tender, 5 to 7 minutes. Stir in the heavy cream, bring to a boil, and then reduce the heat and cook for another 5 to 7 minutes, or until the corn starts to break down and the mixture begins to thicken.

3. Meanwhile, in a large skillet, cook the pancetta until brown and crisp. Transfer to a paper towel–lined plate.

4. Add the pancetta, goat cheese and cheddar to the creamed corn. Season with salt and pepper. Remove the creamed corn from the heat, transfer to a serving dish, and garnish with the parsley and chives before serving.

Rainbow POTATO HASH

LIAM'S CHOICE

We (actually, Liam) came up with a tradition in the McDermott house: Side Dish Meal Night. A dinner comprised entirely of side dishes. Kind of like our version of tapas. The trick is, the side dishes need to be delicious, but they also have to be sturdy enough to stand up on their own. This simple recipe meets that mark in spades. It has all the magic of home fries and can be the perfect Sunday breakfast complement to eggs. But because it's a simple and quick dish to whip up, it is ideal for dinner and is a key player in Side Dish Meal Night.

SERVES 4

1. Fill a large pot with salted water and bring to a boil over high heat. Add all the potatoes, reduce the heat to medium and cook until just fork-tender, 8 to 10 minutes. Drain the potatoes well and set aside.

2. Heat the butter and oil in a large cast-iron skillet over medium heat, and sauté the onions for 2 minutes. Add the garlic and red pepper flakes and sauté for 1 minute.

3. Increase the heat to medium-high and add the potatoes to the skillet. Season with salt and pepper. Cook the potatoes, flipping occasionally with a wide spatula, until they are slightly crispy, 8 to 10 minutes. Transfer the potato hash to a serving dish, garnish with the mint and parsley, and serve at once.

- 2 cups diced red potatoes
- 2 cups diced Yukon Gold potatoes
- 1 cup diced purple potatoes
- 2 tablespoons butter
- 1 tablespoon olive oil
- 1 yellow onion, peeled and diced
- 2 cloves garlic, peeled and minced
- 1/2 to 1 teaspoon crushed red pepper flakes
- Salt and black pepper, to taste
- 2 tablespoons sliced fresh mint, for garnish
- 2 tablespoons chopped fresh parsley, for garnish

Chapter eight

THE SWEET STUFF

D'oh!

I'll never forget the feeling of intense anticipation as I loitered around the oven, waiting for my mom's famous butter tarts to be done. It was torturous watching the brown sugar, butter and raisin filling bubble up and over a beautiful golden brown crust and sizzle as it hit the hot muffin pan. Butter-tart goodness filled the air and made me forget any and all problems, bullies, school tests and all the rest. Those tarts truly were heaven on earth. And aside from the box cakes my mom and I would make together, butter tarts were the only dessert she ever made.

I'd give my left arm to be able to sit in that tiny kitchen again. Hanging out with my mom, a glass of cold milk in one hand, burning the crap out of the roof of my mouth on those butter tarts and sharing a laugh or two. I'll never forget those memories, and I'll never stop yearning for them or experiences that bring them back to me.

In my mind, that's what really makes a great dessert; it is as much about having fond memories as it is about eating something sweet. I think most everyone has a dessert that's all wrapped up in memories. The apple brown Betty your grandmother made every time you came to visit, the pecan pie that finished off Thanksgiving dinner every year, or that specially requested sweet for your birthday.

I'm able to create those memories with my own family now. I share my mom's butter tart recipe with them and tell them stories of Grandma McDermott and how she made me laugh, feel special and, most of all, feel loved. I pass on these recipes with the idea that one day my kids will do the same with their kids. Maybe they'll make a bad day seem much better with my salted caramel ice cream. Perhaps they'll heal a little boy's first broken heart with my quick biscuit doughnuts, or even my mom's butter tarts. So courtesy of my family traditions, from me to you, from you to your kids, from your kids to their kids, and so on, start the mixer, get the sugar and flour out, and let the memories begin.

MY MOM'S BUTTER TARTS
with Vanilla Bean Ice Cream

If apple pie is the most truly "American" dessert, the butter tart is Canada's own national sweet. We've had countrywide contests to find the best recipe, there's a Butter Tart Festival and, heck, there's even the Butter Tart Trail (perfect for hiking after a big dessert) in Wellington North, Ontario. But more than all that is the memory etched in my mind of my mom baking up her signature dessert. It's pretty much just dough and butter and sugar. But it's so much more. Walk into the kitchen on a cold day to the delicate, sweet, rich smell of butter tarts baking, and you'll have an idea of what heaven is like. That smell was one of the very best parts of my childhood. Like a good Canadian woman, my mom made butter tarts that were the sugary equivalent of a hug. If you ever come across a kid who doesn't like butter tarts, check their ID. They're an imposter. But play it safe by leaving out the bourbon in the filling.

MAKES ABOUT 12 INDIVIDUAL TARTS

1. In a food processor, pulse the flour and salt until well blended. Add the butter and pulse until the mixture is crumbly and resembles small frozen peas. Add the shortening and pulse a few times to incorporate.

2. In a small bowl, whisk together the egg, 2 tablespoons ice-cold water and vinegar. Pour the egg mixture slowly into the food processor while pulsing, and process just until the dough begins to pull together and clump. Turn the dough out onto a lightly floured surface and gently coax it together, incorporating any dry pieces. Form the dough into a disk. Wrap it in plastic wrap and refrigerate for at least 30 minutes.

3. In a medium saucepan over medium-high heat, combine the butter, brown sugar and cream for the filling. Stir until the butter is melted and the sugar is completely dissolved, and then remove the saucepan from the heat. Let the mixture cool for a few minutes. Whisk in the egg, bourbon and salt. Stir in the pecans.

4. Preheat the oven to 400°F.

5. Roll the chilled dough out on a floured surface to ⅛-inch thick and use a biscuit cutter to cut 4-inch circles. Press a circle of dough down into each of the wells of a 12-cup muffin tin, and then pour the filling in until each well is three-quarters full.

Dough

1½ cups all-purpose flour

¼ teaspoon salt

6 tablespoons unsalted butter, frozen and cubed

2 tablespoons vegetable shortening, frozen and cubed

1 large egg

1 teaspoon vinegar

Filling

⅛ cup unsalted butter

¾ cup packed brown sugar

3 tablespoons heavy cream

1 large egg

2 tablespoons bourbon

½ teaspoon salt

½ cup toasted and chopped pecans

6. Bake until the tarts are golden and bubbly, 10 to 15 minutes. Cool them in the muffin tin for 5 minutes. Then immediately loosen the edges of the tarts with a thin-bladed knife and gently rotate them in the muffin tin to prevent sticking. Cool for a few more minutes before removing from the muffin tin.

7. Serve the butter tarts warm with a scoop of your favorite vanilla bean ice cream.

APPLE PIE *without Some Cheese* *Is like a Kiss without a Squeeze*

MY MOM'S FAVE

On the rare occasion when we had apple pie, it was usually brought over by a friend or family. I would sit there with my slice of pie and ice cream, dumbfounded as I watched my mom slice a big ole piece of cheddar cheese, put it on top of her pie, pop it under the broiler, wait until it was all bubbly and gooey, and dig in. With a big grin on her face, she would say, "Apple pie without some cheese is like a kiss without a squeeze." I was horrified at the thought of my mom kissing, but more so about the cheese on pie. It wasn't until I was thirteen—when I got my first kiss—that I decided to try cheddar cheese on apple pie. Turns out, I love both of them, and haven't stopped since. Just cut a small piece of cheddar and put it on the side for the kids. If they like it, great. If not, more for you!

2 tablespoons granulated sugar

½ teaspoon ground cinnamon

3 tablespoons unsalted butter, plus 4 tablespoons for the filling

One 14-ounce box refrigerated premade pie crust dough

½ cup shredded cheddar cheese

3 Granny Smith apples, peeled, cored and cut into ¼-inch slices

Zest of 1 small lemon

SERVES 6

1. Preheat the oven to 350°F.

2. In a small bowl, whisk together the sugar and cinnamon, set aside. In a small pot over medium heat, melt 3 tablespoons of the butter.

3. Cut the premade dough into six 2-inch by 3-inch rectangles. Space out evenly on a cookie sheet and gently prick the crusts with a fork to keep them from puffing. Brush each crust with melted butter.

4. Bake until the crusts are slightly golden on the underside, about 10 minutes. Sprinkle with the cheddar cheese and bake for 3 to 5 minutes, or until golden brown and the cheese is melted. Remove and let cool.

5. In a sauté pan over medium-high heat, melt 2 tablespoons of butter. Sauté half of the apples until soft and slightly browned, about 4 minutes. Sprinkle with about a quarter of the sugar-and-cinnamon mixture and set aside. Repeat with the remaining apples.

6. Place a pie crust on a dessert plate, sprinkle with about a sixth of the remaining sugar mixture, and spoon warm apples over the crust. Top with a scoop of vanilla ice cream if desired, and a pinch of lemon zest. Repeat with the rest of the crusts.

GRILLED POUND CAKE
with Berries and Syllabub

Tori sometimes calls me "Grill Boy," because I use my grill so much. But when you have great weather and a nice big grill, why not? So I made a dessert with grilled pound cake. Before you go turning up your nose, you need to taste it. Grilling brings out the sweetness of just about anything, especially a pound cake. I combine this unusual twist with a delicacy pulled from the pages of history. Syllabub is a funny-sounding, centuries-old traditional English dessert. Basically, it's sweetened curdled milk or cream. I know it doesn't sound quite as lovely as whipped cream, but know this—you curdle it with booze! The result is a treat full of sweet, rich flavor. Combine all that sweetness with the natural goodness of berries in season (or frozen berries when they're not), and you have a knockout dessert. Oh, did I mention this was the dessert on my winning menu for *Rachael vs. Guy*? The one that got Guy Fieri his first win?

SERVES 4 TO 6

1. Preheat a grill over medium-low, or heat a grill pan over medium-high heat.

2. In a large bowl, combine the berries and the red wine. Refrigerate for at least 1 hour.

3. Meanwhile, cut the pound cake into 1½-inch slices. Brush both sides of each slice with the butter and sprinkle with the brown sugar. Grill each slice until golden and etched with sear marks, 30 seconds to 1 minute per side. (Avoid moving the slices more than necessary.) Set aside.

4. In a small bowl, whisk together the granulated sugar, sherry, brandy and vanilla until the sugar is almost dissolved.

5. In the bowl of a mixer fitted with a whisk attachment, beat the heavy cream, slowly adding the sugar mixture. Beat until soft peaks form. Cover and refrigerate until you are ready to assemble the dessert.

6. Arrange the grilled pound cake slices on a platter so that they overlap. Spoon the berries over the cake slices with a slotted spoon and top with heaping spoonfuls of the syllabub (whipped cream mixture). Garnish with the basil.

1 pound mixed fresh blackberries, raspberries and strawberries (strawberries quartered and hulled)

2 cups hearty red wine (preferably Cabernet Sauvignon)

1 pound cake (store-bought or your favorite homemade recipe)

2 tablespoons unsalted butter, softened

2 tablespoons brown sugar

3 tablespoons granulated sugar

2 tablespoons sherry

1 tablespoon brandy

1 teaspoon pure vanilla extract

1 cup heavy cream

6 fresh basil leaves, sliced, for garnish

FOR THE kiddos

Even though it would be nice to get the kids to bed early, you need to cut out the alcohol in this recipe. Instead, mix the berries with 2 tablespoons sugar and 1 tablespoon lemon juice, and refrigerate for at least an hour. Whip the cream with 1 tablespoon sugar and ½ teaspoon vanilla until stiff peaks form. Then get out the novelty cookie cutter. I use a circle cutter to make clown faces out of the pound cake, with berries for the eyes and nose (and a berry bow tie), and dollops of whipped cream as the hair. Use food coloring and streak the hair in wild colors, and tell the kids to devour the clowns. Or make animals if you want to avoid any potential clown nightmares!

Cracked Pink Peppercorn and Strawberry
CHEESECAKE WITH A BISCOTTI CRUST

Before the wolf pack came along, Tori and I loved to go out for dinner. We especially liked trying new restaurants, and our favorite desserts were the ones that daringly combined unusual ingredients. I came up with this dessert in the spirit of unexpected unions, combining a lightly savory flavor with enticing sweetness. It may seem a little bizarre at first glance, but pink peppercorns aren't really peppercorns. They are actually the small berries of a shrub, are not nearly as peppery as black peppercorns and have a very understated flowery flavor. I use a New York–style cheesecake instead of a ricotta-based Italian version, because when you have a complex blend of flavors, it's best to go with a simple, smooth texture. And the crust is to die for—a major upgrade over the basic, bland graham cracker variety.

SERVES 8 TO 10

1. Preheat the oven to 350°F. Grease a 9-inch springform pan with butter.

2. Prepare the strawberry topping. Combine all the ingredients for the strawberry topping in a medium saucepan. Bring to a boil over medium-high heat, and then reduce the heat and simmer for 4 to 5 minutes, or until the berries soften. Cool and then refrigerate. (The topping can be made in advance and kept in the refrigerator for up to 3 days.)

3. In a small bowl, mix together all the crust ingredients until thoroughly incorporated. Evenly distribute the biscotti mixture over the bottom of the prepared springform pan and press it with the back of a spoon to ensure an even thickness. Place the springform pan in the freezer and chill.

4. Meanwhile, prepare the filling. In the bowl of a mixer fitted with a paddle attachment, beat the cream cheese until smooth and creamy. With the mixer running, slowly pour in 1¼ cups of the sugar and beat until entirely incorporated.

5. Add the eggs one at a time. Scrape down the sides of the bowl after each egg is added. Add the ground peppercorns and the salt, mixing until incorporated.

6. Pour the filling into the chilled crust. Bake until just set, but still slightly jiggly, 45 to 55 minutes. Remove to a wire rack and cool

Strawberry Topping

2 cups hulled and quartered fresh strawberries (or substitute frozen strawberries off-season)

Juice of 1 orange

Juice of 1 small lemon

2 tablespoons granulated sugar

2 tablespoons balsamic vinegar

½ teaspoon orange zest

½ teaspoon lemon zest

Crust

2 cups almond biscotti crumbs

5 tablespoons unsalted butter, melted

2 tablespoons granulated sugar

½ teaspoon salt

Filling

2 pounds cream cheese, at room temperature

1¼ cups granulated sugar, plus ¼ cup for the crème fraîche

4 large eggs, at room temperature

1 tablespoon coarsely ground pink peppercorns, plus 1½ teaspoons cracked for garnish

¼ teaspoon salt

⅔ cup crème fraîche

Juice and zest of 1 small lemon

10 fresh mint leaves, for garnish

6 fresh basil leaves, sliced, for garnish

completely, about 4 hours. When the cheesecake is completely cool, remove from the springform pan.

7. In a small bowl, whisk together the crème fraîche, the remaining ¼ cup sugar, and the lemon juice and zest. Spread this over the top of the cooled cheescake. Cover the cheesecake with plastic and refrigerate overnight, or for at least 5 hours.

8. Serve slices of the cheesecake with a heaping spoonful of the strawberry topping. Garnish with the remaining cracked peppercorns, the mint and basil.

FOR THE kiddos

When it comes to desserts for children, I go the individual-serving route to head off any "She got more than I did" moments. Make the cheesecake filling and crust just as you would with the adult version, with the exception of the pink peppercorns. Use biscuit or round cookie cutters as small cheesecake molds. Butter the cookie cutters, arrange them on a baking sheet and press the crust mixture into the base of each. Fill each mold three-quarters full with filling and bake until golden, 15 to 20 minutes. Cool the cheesecakes completely on the counter and then refrigerate them in the molds overnight. Carefully remove the molds and garnish the cheesecakes with whipped cream and the Strawberry Topping. I'd suggest you make extra of these little cheesecakes, because they are mega-favorites of kids (and wannabe kids) everywhere.

ARBORIO RICE PUDDING
with Toasted Almond Chocolate Ganache

I don't know if there is one absolutely perfectly sweet treat out there, but ganache is as close to it as you're likely to ever get. Ganache is a velvety, intensely chocolaty icing, glaze or filling (depending on the ratio of cream to chocolate). I swear, I'd eat my hand if it were covered in ganache—which is why I'm very careful when working with it. And almonds are a perfect accent to the richness of the chocolate. All those rich flavors can be pretty intense, so I've partnered them with a pudding made from short-grain, starchy arborio rice that is a little like risotto. It adds the perfect body and texture, and low-key flavor.

SERVES 6

1. Place the chocolate in a medium heatproof mixing bowl. In a small saucepan over medium-high heat, bring the cream to a boil. Pour the hot cream over the chocolate and let it stand for 10 minutes, or until the chocolate is nearly melted. Whisk the mixture, thoroughly incorporating the cream into the chocolate.

2. Stir in the salt and then pour the ganache into a shallow baking dish. Refrigerate the ganache until it is firm enough to scoop, 30 to 45 minutes.

3. Melt the butter in a large saucepan over medium heat. Add the rice and toast for 2 to 3 minutes, or until it just begins to brown. Add the brown sugar, cinnamon and salt, and stir to coat the rice evenly.

4. Add the almond milk to the saucepan, increase the heat and bring to a boil. Reduce the heat and simmer, uncovered, stirring occasionally, until the rice is puffed and tender, 25 to 30 minutes. (Use a little more almond milk if you prefer a runnier rice pudding. Four cups makes a creamy texture.)

5. While the pudding cooks, scoop the stiffened ganache into 1-inch balls using a melon baller or spoon. Roll each ball in the chopped almonds. Refrigerate until ready to serve.

6. Spoon the warm pudding into individual bowls, place a ganache ball in each bowl of pudding and sprinkle with freshly ground cinnamon.

Ganache

8 ounces semisweet chocolate, coarsely chopped

½ cup heavy cream

¼ teaspoon salt

½ cup toasted and finely chopped almonds

Pudding

2 tablespoons unsalted butter

1 cup arborio rice

½ cup brown sugar

½ teaspoon ground cinnamon

½ teaspoon salt

4 to 5 cups almond milk

1 cinnamon stick, ground

Dean's Food 411

Toasting almonds and other nuts is a fantastic way to bring out the flavor and personality of the nuts. It's also super easy. You can even use this method for toasting pine nuts (incredible on salads) or other nuts. Toast the almonds on the stove in a heavy, dry skillet over medium heat. Move the nuts around constantly until golden brown. Don't let them sit, and don't toast them too long, or they'll burn. As an alternative, toast nuts on a baking sheet in a 350°F oven. They'll take about 8 to 10 minutes, and you should stir them every couple of minutes. I prefer the stovetop method myself, because with a pack of little "nuts" running around, it's way too easy to forget that there are nuts are in the oven.

Apple-and-Cinnamon
ICE CREAM PIE

JACK'S CHOICE

I'm not the one who makes the rules, so I can't tell exactly why apples and ice cream go together so well, but they do. Throw cinnamon into the mix, and you've got an absolute winner. It doesn't hurt to pile that mix into a lovely lightly spiced graham cracker crust. It's sort of like apple pie à la mode with the à la mode built right in. If you want to get all fancy, use a totally different ice cream. Something like *dulce de leche* could definitely switch it up a bit and add a whole new element of super sweetness to this delicious dessert.

SERVES 4 TO 6

1. Preheat the oven to 350°F.

2. In a medium bowl, combine the graham crackers for the crust with the melted butter, the sugar, cinnamon, nutmeg and salt and mix well. Spoon the mixture evenly over the bottom of a pie pan and press it with the back of a spoon. Place the crust in the freezer and chill for 10 minutes.

3. Bake the crust until the edges start to brown, 7 to 10 minutes. Remove it from the oven and let it cool to room temperature.

4. Combine the pecans, granola, brown sugar, flour and chilled butter in a medium bowl, and mix with your hands, squeezing the butter between your fingers until fully incorporated. Spread the mixture on a baking sheet, and bake until golden and toasted, 5 to 7 minutes. Remove the streusel from the oven and set aside to cool.

5. Peel, core and dice 2 of the apples. Peel and grate the remaining apple, and toss the grated apple with the lemon juice and zest in a small bowl. Set the diced apples aside.

6. Melt the butter in a large sauté pan over medium-high heat and sauté the diced apples until soft, stirring often. Remove the apples and their juices to a small bowl, sprinkle with the sugar and cinnamon, and let cool.

7. In the bowl of a stand mixer fitted with a paddle attachment, gently whip the ice cream for 1 minute. Fold in the cooked apples and any accumulated juices, the grated apples and the pinch of salt.

8. Spoon the apple-and-cinnamon ice cream into the prepared pie crust, and cover with the streusel topping. Freeze the ice cream pie for at least 8 hours, and preferably overnight, before serving.

Crust

- 2 cups graham cracker crumbs
- 5 tablespoons unsalted butter, melted
- 2 tablespoons granulated sugar
- ½ teaspoon ground cinnamon
- ½ teaspoon ground nutmeg
- ½ teaspoon salt

Streusel Topping

- ¾ cup chopped pecans
- ⅔ cup old-fashioned granola
- ⅔ cup light brown sugar
- ¼ cup all-purpose flour
- 3 tablespoons unsalted butter, chilled and diced

Apple-and-Cinnamon Ice Cream

- 3 Pink Lady apples
- Juice and zest of 1 small lemon
- 2 tablespoons unsalted butter
- ½ cup granulated sugar
- 1 teaspoon ground cinnamon
- ½ gallon vanilla bean ice cream, slightly thawed
- Pinch of salt

VANILLA BEAN PANNA COTTA

TORI'S CHOICE

with Seasonal Fruit & Amaretto Whipped Cream

This is the Italian equivalent of crème brûlée, although a lot of dinner guests have told me that it has no equivalent. There are actually layers of richness, provided by real vanilla right from the source, sweet natural honey and satisfying heavy cream. Using fruit in season adds a big jolt of freshness to the dessert. There's really not much more you could ask from a dessert: sophisticated enough to make a big splash at even a fancy sit-down dinner party, easy enough to make any given weeknight when you want to treat the troops!

SERVES 4 TO 6

1. Pour the milk into a small bowl and sprinkle the gelatin over it. Let the mixture sit for 3 to 5 minutes, allowing the gelatin to activate and "bloom."

2. Combine the cream, honey, vanilla seeds and vanilla pod, and the lemon peel in a small pot and simmer over medium heat for 3 minutes. Stir and scrape the bottom of the pot with a spatula frequently to ensure the cream doesn't scorch.

3. Whisk in the gelatin mixture. Cook, stirring, until the gelatin has fully dissolved, about 1 minute. Remove from the heat and strain the custard mixture through a fine mesh strainer into individual molds, such as custard dishes, small tumblers or—for a fancy presentation—martini glasses or champagne flutes.

4. Allow the custard to cool to room temperature. Then cover and chill in the refrigerator for at least 6 hours, but preferably overnight.

5. In the bowl of a stand mixer with a whisk attachment, combine the cream, Amaretto and honey. Beat on high until soft peaks form. In a small bowl, toss together the mint and cilantro.

6. Serve each panna cotta with a heaping spoonful of fruit, a large dollop of Amaretto whipped cream and a generous sprinkling of biscotti crumbs. Garnish each with mint and cilantro.

Custard

1 cup whole milk

One ¼-ounce packet unflavored gelatin

2 cups heavy cream

½ cup honey

1 vanilla bean, split lengthwise, seeds scraped out, pod and seeds reserved

Peel of 1 lemon

2 cups mixed blackberries, strawberries and blueberries (or substitute fresh seasonal fruit of your choice)

Topping

1 cup heavy cream

1 tablespoon Amaretto liqueur

2 teaspoons honey

¼ cup thinly sliced fresh mint, for garnish

8 thinly sliced fresh cilantro leaves, for garnish

2 almond biscotti, finely crushed

FOR THE kiddos

Let's get individual for the kids. Shrink the panna cotta with some small, unusual and fun containers. I use small juice glasses. You can even make it more individual by adding a drop or two of food coloring to each serving when you pour the panna cotta into the glass. Mix it up a little, and every kid at the table can have his or her own color.

MY FAVORITE BUTTERSCOTCH PUDDING
with Pecan Brittle

The first taste of any butterscotch pudding takes me back to rainy days, or any day I was home sick from school, when my mom made butterscotch pudding. It was the box stuff and not the best I've ever tasted, but it sure made me feel better. My version still takes me back, but it has a much deeper and more complex flavor. There's butterscotch, and then there's *this* butterscotch. One taste of this pudding and the kids will never settle for a boxed version—and neither will you. Throw in a healthy helping of brittle, and you'll never eat butterscotch pudding any other way. Use chopped macadamia nuts, plain old peanuts or any nut that catches your fancy. The brittle is a perfect complement to my very own favorite butterscotch pudding.

SERVES 4 TO 6

1. In a medium saucepan, whisk together the brown sugar, cornstarch and salt for the pudding until thoroughly combined. Slowly whisk in the milk and cream. Place the saucepan over medium-high heat and add the butter. Bring the mixture to a boil and cook, whisking constantly, for 2 minutes.

2. Remove the saucepan from the heat and stir in the rum and vanilla. Pour the hot pudding into ramekins or custard cups and allow to cool to room temperature. Then place plastic wrap directly on the surface of the pudding (to prevent a skin from forming), and chill for at least 3 hours.

3. Line a baking sheet with a nonstick baking mat, such as a Silpat, or with parchment paper that has been sprayed with nonstick cooking spray. Set aside. Grease an offset spatula and set aside.

4. Stir together the sugar, corn syrup and ½ cup water in a large heavy saucepan. Bring to a boil over medium-high heat and cook, swirling the mixture but not stirring, until it reaches 238°F. Add the butter and stir to incorporate. Continue cooking until the mixture reaches 300°F.

5. Stir in the pecan halves, salt and smoked paprika. Remove from the heat and stir in the baking soda. (The mixture will start to foam, indicating that it is properly aerated and the brittle will be light and crispy.) Pour the hot brittle mixture onto the prepared baking sheet and spread it out evenly with the offset spatula. Sprinkle the chopped pecans evenly over the top.

6. Let the brittle cool completely. When it has set completely, crack it into pieces. Serve the butterscotch pudding with pieces of brittle on top.

Pudding

1 cup brown sugar

3 tablespoons cornstarch

1 teaspoon salt

1½ cups whole milk

1 cup heavy cream

4 tablespoons unsalted butter, cut into pats

1 tablespoon dark rum

1 teaspoon pure vanilla extract

Pecan Brittle

2 cups granulated sugar

½ cup light corn syrup

4 tablespoons unsalted butter, cut into pats

2 cups toasted pecan halves, plus ½ cup toasted and finely chopped pecans

1 teaspoon salt

2 teaspoons smoked Spanish paprika

1 teaspoon baking soda

FOR THE **kiddos**

Normally, I don't include anything alcoholic in a kids' dessert, but the rum here is such a small amount and it's so crucial to the flavor that I go ahead and include it. However, leave the paprika out of the brittle. Adults tend to love the unusual spiciness of the brittle, but kids will like it more as a straightforward brittle. Let the kids crack the brittle with the back of a spoon, and let them decorate their own puddings with the shards of yummy goodness.

GRILLED PEACHES
with Whipped Goat Cheese & Honeyed Balsamic

I find that kids and adults alike are fascinated whenever you grill fruit. Grilling intensifies the sweetness of the fruit and in this case really brings out its essential "peachiness." Bonus: Kids love goat cheese!

SERVES 4

1. Preheat your outdoor grill to medium, or heat a grill pan over medium heat.

2. Season the peaches, cut side up, with the brown sugar, thyme, and salt and pepper to taste. Drizzle the oil on the cut sides. Grill the peaches, cut side down, until they are caramelized and golden, 2 to 3 minutes. Gently flip and continue to grill until tender. Set aside.

3. Combine the balsamic vinegar, honey, vanilla bean seeds, the 1 teaspoon of salt and the ¼ teaspoon of pepper in a medium bowl. Whisk while slowly pouring in ⅔ cup of the oil, until thoroughly blended. Set aside.

4. In a small bowl, mix the goat cheese with a fork until smooth. Stir in the lemon zest and set aside.

5. Stir together the lemon juice, the remaining 1 tablespoon oil, salt and pepper, if desired, in a small bowl. Add the arugula and toss to coat.

6. Arrange the arugula on each of 4 salad plates and place 1½ peach halves on top of each. Garnish the peaches with a dollop of whipped goat cheese. Scatter the pecans and mint over each plate. Drizzle with the reserved vinaigrette and serve.

3 ripe peaches, halved and pitted

2 tablespoons light brown sugar

1 tablespoon fresh thyme leaves

1 teaspoon salt, plus more to taste

¼ teaspoon freshly ground black pepper, plus more to taste

1 tablespoon olive oil, for drizzling

⅓ cup balsamic vinegar

2 tablespoons honey

Seeds of 1 vanilla bean (split pod lengthwise and scrape out seeds)

⅔ cup olive oil, plus 1 tablespoon for the arugula

One 4-ounce log goat cheese, at room temperature

Zest and juice of ½ a lemon

20 arugula leaves

¼ cup toasted and coarsely chopped pecans

10 fresh mint leaves, torn

Put a little hip hop in your kids' dinner. Make a bunny face, and you'll amuse young diners at the same time you feed them. Don't be surprised if they ask for more—grilled peaches become a big favorite among budding foodies.

SERVES 2

3 ripe peaches, grilled according to the directions in the adult recipe

10 arugula leaves, stems mostly removed

3 ounces goat cheese

2 tablespoons chopped pecans, plus 4 pecan halves

4 fresh mint leaves, thinly sliced

1   Use 4 of the 6 peach halves to form 2 bunny faces. Slice the fifth peach half in half again to make 2 bunny bodies. Quarter the remaining peach half to make 2 sets of ears.

2   Arrange the arugula on the bottom half of each of 2 plates to make the grass. Place a bunny body in the "grass" on each plate, and top each bunny body with a bunny face (2 peach halves, rounded side up, equal 1 bunny face). Place 2 peach quarters above the face on each plate to form the bunny ears.

3   Slice and roll the goat cheese into four ½-inch balls. Roll the balls in the chopped pecans. Use 2 of the balls for each bunny nose. Use the remaining 4 pecan halves for the eyes, and add the mint to make whiskers.

SEMOLINA SWEET PUDDING
with Strawberry Preserves and Black Pepper–Almond Tuiles

LIAM'S CHOICE

Just about every nation—from India to Greece to Germany—claims credit for semolina pudding. No wonder, because this stuff is straight up delicious. It's also customizable. Everyone has their own preferences, but I make mine sweet, because that's the way the brood likes it, from Tori down to Finn. This is flat-out fun to make, and something the kids can do with no problem.

SERVES 4 TO 6

1. Preheat the oven to 350°F. Line a baking sheet with a nonstick baking mat, such as a Silpat, or aluminum foil.

2. In a medium bowl, whisk together the almond flour, all-purpose flour, ½ cup of the sugar, salt and pepper.

3. In a small bowl, whisk the egg whites until frothy. Add the butter and whisk to combine. Pour the egg-butter mixture into the flour mixture and whisk until just incorporated.

4. Spoon 1 tablespoon mounds of the tuile mixture onto the prepared baking sheet, leaving 4 inches between the mounds. Using the back of a spoon, spread each mound out to form a 3-inch circle. Sprinkle with the almonds and bake until golden, 7 to 10 minutes.

5. Remove the tuiles from the oven and let stand on the baking sheet for 1 minute. Pick each up with a thin metal spatula and gently curve around the underside of a wooden spoon to form a partial tube. The tuiles may crack slightly. (You can make the tuiles ahead of time. They'll last for up to 2 days in an airtight container.)

6. Combine the milk, the remaining ¼ cup sugar and the vanilla in a medium saucepan and cook over medium-high heat, stirring constantly, until the mixture just begins to boil.

7. Whisk in the semolina flour and cinnamon, and reduce the heat to low. Simmer, uncovered, for 5 to 6 minutes, or until the mixture thickens and resembles a porridge.

8. Serve the semolina pudding in shallow bowls, each topped with strawberry preserves and garnished with a tuile.

½ cup almond flour

¼ cup all-purpose flour

½ cup granulated sugar, plus ¼ cup for the pudding

¼ teaspoon salt

1 tablespoon freshly cracked black pepper

2 large egg whites

7 tablespoons unsalted butter, melted and cooled

½ cup toasted and finely chopped almonds

2½ cups whole milk

½ teaspoon pure vanilla extract

½ cup semolina flour

½ teaspoon ground cinnamon

½ cup high-quality strawberry preserves

VINEGAR

Acknowledgments

**Words cannot express my gratitude to the following people
for all their help and creativity...**

Jack, Liam, Stella, Hattie and baby Finn for being my little foodie guinea pigs

Meghan Prophet, you started it all

Food Network U.S. and Canada

Guy Fieri and Rachael Ray

Chris Peterson for always being there when I needed you

James Tse, for your creative genius

Claudia and Jason

My manager, Robert Flutie, for your friendship, love and belief in me

Jane Dystel and Miriam Goderich for believing in this book

Everyone at Harlequin for helping me make The Gourmet Dad *vision come to life,
and being so amazingly great to work with*

Rebecca Hunt for guiding me through my first book

*And again my two angels: Mom and Tori. One watches over me from above,
and the other forever by my side. I love you*

Dean

X O X O

Recipes followed by an asterisk include a Kids' Version.